Let your creativity flow...

- Inspirations From
Eastern Counties Vol II
Edited by Steve Twelvetree

 Young**Writers**

First published in Great Britain in 2005 by:
Young Writers
Remus House
Coltsfoot Drive
Peterborough
PE2 9JX
Telephone: 01733 890066
Website: www.youngwriters.co.uk

SB ISBN 1 84602 227 4

Foreword

Young Writers was established in 1991 and has been passionately devoted to the promotion of reading and writing in children and young adults ever since. The quest continues today. Young Writers remains as committed to the fostering of burgeoning poetic and literary talent as ever.

This year's Young Writers competition has proven as vibrant and dynamic as ever and we are delighted to present a showcase of the best poetry from across the UK. Each poem has been carefully selected from a wealth of *Playground Poets* entries before ultimately being published in this, our thirteenth primary school poetry series.

Once again, we have been supremely impressed by the overall high quality of the entries we have received. The imagination, energy and creativity which has gone into each young writer's entry made choosing the best poems a challenging and often difficult but ultimately hugely rewarding task - the general high standard of the work submitted amply vindicating this opportunity to bring their poetry to a larger appreciative audience.

We sincerely hope you are pleased with our final selection and that you will enjoy *Playground Poets - Inspirations From Eastern Counties Vol II* for many years to come.

Contents

Manea Community School, Manea

Charlotte Kerr (10)	30
Daniel McDermott (9)	30
Jamie Francis (11)	31
Ashley Bridgement (9)	31
Stevie Harrow (8)	31
Dan Sansom (11)	32
Callum Baker (10)	32
Asia Fox (9)	33
Sarah Day (11)	33
Kelly Howell (9)	33
Jake Winter (9)	34
Louisha Connolly (11)	34
Caitlin Wilby (9)	34
Conner Howell (9)	35
Leanne Spry (11)	35
Kieran Howell (9)	35
Sharon Howell (11)	36
Suzanne Larham (11)	36
Jack Lilley (11)	37
Georgina Fitzgibbon (10)	37
Jaimee-Leigh Webb (10)	37
Nikki Hopkin (10)	38
George Burton (10)	38
Daniel Davies (11)	38
Kate Baxter (9)	39
George McCarthy (11)	39
Shanice Setchfield (10)	39
Adam Fenn (9)	40
Darcy Attrill (10)	40
Ashley Bullman (8)	40
Courtney Milner (11)	41
Rebecca Lawrence (10)	41
Abbie Burridge (10)	41
Ryan Spry (9)	42

Middlefield CP School, Eynesbury

Naomi Adams (10)	42
Daniella Chapman (9)	43
Brady Mayes (11)	43
Rebecca Riley-Brown (9)	44

Nicola Taylor (10)	61
Jenny Kent (11)	61
Lucy Hitchcock (10)	62
Joanna Leader (10)	62
Cressida Rigney (11)	63
Emma Marriott (11)	63
Megan Gilligan (11)	64
Megan Parkins (11)	64
Antonia Foster (11)	64
Alex Sutcliffe (11)	65
Kitty Underwood (11)	65
Charlotte Jeanroy (11)	66

Wendover CE Junior School, Wendover

Timothy Castling (8)	66
Orie Amadi (8)	67
Jack Wells (8)	67
Tom Bedwell (8)	67
Ella Wallis (8)	68
Charlotte Atkins (8)	68
Zoe Freeman (11)	69
Robin Geddes (7)	69
Samuel Pring (11)	70
Amy McKay (11)	70
Emma Donald (10)	71
Sarah Patton (10)	71
Alex McGowan (11)	72
Kane Pril (11)	72
Emily Davies-Hawes (10)	73
Charlotte Grimsdale (11)	73
Alys Reed (9)	74
Jack Williamson (9)	74
Louisa Down (11)	75
Ellen Blackburn (10)	75
Emily Hogg (11)	76
Lauren Halpin (11)	76
Eleanor Fenner (10)	77
James Edmonds (11)	77
Hayley Morgan (9)	78
Elena Marris (10)	78
Georgie Wilton (9)	78

Josh Bailey (11)	79
Chloe Coggins (11)	79
Rory Griffiths (10) & Faisal Khan (9)	80
Rebecca McCleary (11)	80
Helen Dawson (10)	81
Zack Saunders (10)	81
Calum Findlay & Brett Collings (10)	82
Shannon Skidmore (8)	83
Jason Gooderham (10)	83
Joseph Hodson (9)	84
Ben Geddes (10)	84
Tom Erlandsen (10)	85
Georgina Kerr (8)	85
Daniel Patton (8)	86
Amy Simpson & Jayde Paxton (10)	86
Aimee Grice (11)	87
Callum Lawes (10)	87
Bou Man Lau (9)	88
Kate Thompson (11)	88
Sarah Jane Wilkinson (9)	88
Kieran Bendix (11)	89
Leonora Lawrence (10)	89
Daniel Geddes (9)	89
Lucy Sigley (9)	90
Nathan McCleary (11)	90
Sophie Honeyball (11)	90
Natasha Pain (9)	91
Jessica Timlin (11)	91
Rebecca Bailey (11)	92
Rebecca Noall (11)	92
Klara Hommel (8)	92
Oliver Gunson (7)	93
Lauren Baker (11)	93
Joshua Davies (10)	94
Andrew Howarth (10)	94
Annabel Taswell-Fryer (7)	95
Milly Collier (11)	95
Charlotte Dyer (9)	96
Thomas Robertson (11)	96
Harry Stroud (8)	97
Orla Flynn (11)	97
Rachel Durrant (10)	98

William Austin Junior School, Luton

The Poems

Fear

Fear is like black darkness everywhere.
Fear sounds like people screaming.
Like a herd of cows coming to get you.
Fear tastes like burning ashes spreading around the cold room.
It smells like chickens running through the forest.
Fear looks like rotten bodies curled up like sausage rolls.
It feels like someone chasing you.
It reminds you of a volcano exploding like a blasting fire.

Iram Ishaq (11)
Beech Hill Community Primary School, Luton

What Can You See?

The wicked silver convertible, on full speed,
Dodging all the other gigantic trucks.
The convertible's windows were shining like a diamond ring.
The lights were flashing so bright
That they looked even brighter than the sun.
The roaring engine made a very loud noise
That was even worse than the noise of an air raid.

Sajid Khurshid (11)
Beech Hill Community Primary School, Luton

Sad Poetry

Sadness is like the silver bright sea.
It sounds like someone screaming from a mile away.
It tastes like raw chicken mixed with cold oil.
Smells like death from far away.
Looks like a bottomless pit filled with darkness for eternity.
Feels like a fierce hyena ripping you apart.
Reminds me of death getting closer like a lion ready to pounce.

Bashar Abedin (10)
Beech Hill Community Primary School, Luton

Love

Love is as red as a beautiful rose in its bed
It sounds like the deep blue sea coming towards the
shore calmly at night
It tastes like a cake covered in chocolate with cream
It smells like red perfume waiting to be used
It reminds me of my family.

Masswar Mahmood (11)
Beech Hill Community Primary School, Luton

Sad Poetry

Sad is like a black sky which is twisting down to me.
It sounds like rain dropping from the sky and flooding my country.
It tastes like the candy-filled Zapper
Which is sour and bitter to me.
It smells like poisonous venom gas which would kill me.
It looks like a brown tornado chasing me.
It feels like a dark, evil soul which is going to execute my bones,
It reminds me of the sky when I fell and died.

Juten Ahmed (11)
Beech Hill Community Primary School, Luton

My Emotions

I hate it when I lose things like money,
I am surprised when every day is sunny,
I get angry when people do things that aren't funny,
I like it when I get to go somewhere with my family.

I hate it when today is a bad day,
I am surprised when May is my birthday,
I get angry when people won't let me play,
I like it when I eat my favourite food without delay.

Hazeq Khalid (11)
Beech Hill Community Primary School, Luton

Laughter

Laughter is as gold as a shiny and gleaming jewellery set.
It sounds like a bunch of hyenas laughing
As if they've been given a tasty meal to eat.
It tastes like chocolate-flavoured ice cream melting in your mouth,
Sweet, getting ready to tickle you.
It smells like chips flowing through the air,
Ready to get into your stomach.
It feels like warm water running all over you.
It reminds you of going to the funfair,
Playing like a little kid on the rides.

Tanjina Jahan (11)
Beech Hill Community Primary School, Luton

What Can You See In War?

I can see people getting shot by guns.
I can see people filling their tanks with oil.
I can see children crying because their families are dead.
I can see planes dropping bombs.

Nassir Khan (11)
Beech Hill Community Primary School, Luton

A Story Of Love

Love is like the colour of a red boat floating through a tunnel of love.
It sounds like the birds singing through the trees in the morning light.
It tastes like sugar that you can't get enough of.
Love smells like a pink perfume waiting to be used.
It looks like a flower blooming in the springtime.
Love feels like a magical spell put on you by fairies from the love queen.
Love reminds me of a chocolate flake floating in my eyes.

Abdul Subhan Rasul (11)
Beech Hill Community Primary School, Luton

Sad

Sadness is blue like a rolling sea.
It sounds like starving children crying.
It tastes like sour milk, sweet as chocolate milkshake.
It looks like rain pouring from the white sky.
It feels like being chased by a herd of elephants.
It reminds me of a miserable, dark day.

Yasmin Sultana (11)
Beech Hill Community Primary School, Luton

What Can You Feel In The War?

I can feel we are going to lose the war.
I can feel my blood squirting everywhere.
I can feel thunder crashing above me.
I can feel my head sweating and the bullet is going to hit me.

Monzur Ahmed (11)
Beech Hill Community Primary School, Luton

Fear

Fear is dark and black like a scary storeroom.
It sounds like a moaning, groaning sound coming
                              from a scary cemetery.
It tastes like horrible things in your mouth.
It smells like ashes in your backyard.
It looks like a fierce hyena just about to pounce on your teacher.
It feels like a terrible, cold chamber.

Abdul Wahhaab (11)
Beech Hill Community Primary School, Luton

Silence

Silence is as quiet as a mouse tiptoeing,
It sounds like air floating through space.
It tastes like water that is as bland as air.
It smells like ice that is so cold it will make you freeze.
It feels like a blizzard slamming against your face.
It reminds me of my fear growing within like a beast ready to emerge.

Junaid Hussain (9)
Beech Hill Community Primary School, Luton

Silence

Silence is black like the pitch of the night sky.
Silence sounds like the end of time where a single move couldn't be heard.
It tastes like Coke as if it was dried up.
It smells like burnt rubber as if it was on fire.
Silence looks like the solar system with no stars, planets, no moon and no sun.
Silence feels like the wind blowing in your face.
Silence reminds me of death, as vampires take over your soul.

Mustakim Ali (10)
Beech Hill Community Primary School, Luton

What Am I?

I feel like a sharp hedgehog except with leaves.
I taste like tea which is much too sweet.
I look like a mask which was made by a person for his task.
I smell like a flower with its scent livening up the room.
I sound like a drum which keeps going boom.

Amina Khan (11)
Beech Hill Community Primary School, Luton

I Like It When . . .

I like it when we do fun subjects like art,
I hate it when we get a lot of homework,
I am surprised when I get a lot of pocket money for my birthday
And I am angry when I get in trouble for no reason.

I like it when I beat my enemies in football,
I hate it when my sister does not let me watch cartoons,
I am surprised when I do not have to walk to school
And I am angry when I lose something very expensive
and precious to me.

Aminur Rahman (10)
Beech Hill Community Primary School, Luton

The Black Angel

Running through the endless black,
Never turning or looking back,
But up ahead, what's that I see?
A light,
A candle, it may be.
Nearer, nearer,
Bigger, bigger.
I think, I think . . .
My Lord?

Anna Hands (10)
Fulbourn Primary School, Fulbourn

Heather

There was a young lady called Heather
Who did not always like the weather
One day at home
She slipped on a scone
And blamed it all on the weather.

Heather Harper (8)
Great & Little Shelford CE School, Great Shelford

Titanic

Attractive boat,
Couldn't stay afloat.

Iceberg it hits,
Splits in two bits.

Mass killer,
Water spiller.

Found Monday, dead,
Everyone said

It was unsinkable,
Totally unsinkable.

But,
It sank!

It is . . . the Titanic!

Nathalie Botcherby (11)
Great & Little Shelford CE School, Great Shelford

What Is A . . . Ghost?

A ghost is a gust of wind
It is a shiver down the spine
It is a white-coated monster
That walks around at night
It is the creaking of a door
A high-pitched groaning moan
Coming from your cupboard door.

Sophia Christodoulou (11)
Great & Little Shelford CE School, Great Shelford

The Man From Rye

There was a man from Rye
Who kept on eating cow pie
He got so fat
He broke his back
So then he returned to Rye.

Calum Barlow (8)
Great & Little Shelford CE School, Great Shelford

What A Silly Little Green Elf

There was a little green elf,
Who wanted to live on a shelf,
The shelf was too high,
So he started to cry,
What a silly little green elf.

Katie Pullen (8)
Great & Little Shelford CE School, Great Shelford

The Dog And Ellie

There was a young girl called Ellie
Who had a dog that was rather smelly
He went outside
And there he died
And that was the end of Ellie.

Ellie Woodley (7)
Great & Little Shelford CE School, Great Shelford

Dover

There was a person from Dover,
Who rushed through a field of clover,
When some very large bees
Stung his nose and his knees,
So he went back to Dover.

Clodie Mackay (7)
Great & Little Shelford CE School, Great Shelford

That Stupid Young Person From Dundee

There was a young person from Dundee
Who couldn't climb a tree
He tried again and again
And got a great big pain
That stupid young person from Dundee.

Hanna Warne (8)
Great & Little Shelford CE School, Great Shelford

Colours!

Our world is made of colours
They surround us, they're everywhere
They give us joy and happiness throughout the year
No colour is the same, they always change
Colours tell a story, the story of your life!
They take you through your strife
They are your life!

Holly Butcher (11)
Great & Little Shelford CE School, Great Shelford

Wonders Of Egypt

The blazing sun,
the bright blue sea,
the river flows on.
Boats going up stream
and things floating in the river.
Lots of people out in the daytime,
busy taking water and food
on their heads with a basket.

They have gigantic sandy pyramids,
as far as the eye can see.
Huge sandy deserts all around.
The Nile gets flooded
each and every year.
Ducks and swans swim near shore,
the Nile stays alive.
The power of the single god,
A wonderful and ancient land.

Jordon Smyth (9)
Leighton Primary School, Orton Malborne

Water

(Inspired by 'Weather is Full of the Nicest Sounds' by Aileen Fisher)

What makes the strangest sounds . . .

It rumbles and tumbles
It crashes and bashes
It plips and plops
It winkles and tinkles
It drips and drops
It swishes and swashes
It twings and sings
And thrashes and lashes
Water makes the strangest sounds.

Kirsty Croft (7)
Leighton Primary School, Orton Malborne

The Nile

Flowing through Egypt
Sparkling and twinkling
The hot sun
Reflecting on the water
The people
Gathering the reeds
The boats sailing up and down.

Megan Connolley (8)
Leighton Primary School, Orton Malborne

Flowers

Petals delicate and smooth
Beautiful and soft
Swaying in the morning breeze
Twinkling and swirling
As they gleam in the sun
Exploding into a blaze of colour
Tempting for the exploring bees
Searching for the hidden nectar.

Shenna Haynes (9)
Leighton Primary School, Orton Malborne

The River Nile

The sun reflects
On the Nile
Glimmering and shining
As it floats along
People fishing
Boats sailing
Ducks swimming
On the river.

Cody Harris (8)
Leighton Primary School, Orton Malborne

Tutankhamun

A trembling hand
An anxious wait
A small hole
A terrorising tomb
A blasting surprise
A musty smell
A damp floor
A glint of gold
A humongous tomb
A sticky touch
An amazing discovery
A brilliant archaeologist
A powerful force
A statue of animals
A smell of flowers
A sound of whispers
A remarkable adventure
A strange animal with another beside
An exciting mutter.

Katie Harber (9)
Leighton Primary School, Orton Malborne

Spooky Mummies

Washed
in scented oils,
Wrapped
in linen bandages,
Lying
in a tomb,
covered with a mask,
Travelled
to the afterlife.
Spooky mummies.

Matthew Curme (8)
Leighton Primary School, Orton Malborne

Flower

Slim, spiky stem
Stunning star-shaped flower
Silky, smooth petals
Secret stores of pollen
Sweet-smelling lavender
Curvy, crispy, crunchy leaves
Colour, charming
Multicoloured petals
Stem curved like a rainbow
See-through, compact leaves
Delicate, dainty petals like a dress
Drift in the wind
Dreamily dancing at dawn
Dead flowers all floppy and crispy
Silky seeds ready to sprout in spring.

Jack Horton-Williams (8)
Leighton Primary School, Orton Malborne

Sarcophagus

At last it's been found,
Hidden in box after box.
Beautifully decorated,
With gold and coloured glass.
A pharaoh clutching
A sceptre and a flail,
A magnificent death mask,
Pure gold shines in every part
Of the sarcophagus.
A priceless treasure,
Hidden for thousands of years.
Tutankhamun has been found.

Ben Bewick (8)
Leighton Primary School, Orton Malborne

The Sun

So important
Calls himself the boss
Master of everywhere
King of the solar system
Watches all the planets
As they work for him
Mercury dashes round him
Venus is his glamorous maid
Colourful Earth makes him laugh
Mars turns his enemies to blood
The red eye of Jupiter
Stares at his beauty
Saturn entertains him
With his swirling rings
Uranus and Neptune lazily loll about
Pluto so far out, the sun can't see
If he's working or not
The sun
Calls himself the boss
Master of everywhere
King of the solar system.

Emma Scothern (7)
Leighton Primary School, Orton Malborne

Tutankhamun's Tomb

Waiting to be found,
It took six long years.
Four rooms filled with treasure.
Charming gold
And cheerful blue,
Glimmering and sparkling,
As far as the eye can see.
Tutankhamun's treasure
Has been found.

Laura Howard (8)
Leighton Primary School, Orton Malborne

Pompeii

A rumble and a tumble
Rocks falling down
Mount Vesuvius has attacked the town
People screaming from far away
Mount Vesuvius has ruled the day
Gas floating down the hill
Many people were killed
The day Pompeii disappeared.

Bethany Paul
Leighton Primary School, Orton Malborne

Mummy

M any thousands of years ago,
U nder the hot, blaring sun,
M elting people's flesh and blood,
M any gods were worshipped,
Y ellow pyramids were built for burying pharaohs.

Shamraiz Najeeb & Daniel Batty (9)
Leighton Primary School, Orton Malborne

Pyramids

P haraohs ruled the land of Egypt
Y ellow rocks on top of the pyramids
R iver Nile floods the land
A ncient facts you'll start to know
M ummies were created
I n those Egyptian days
D iamonds are very special
S everal treasures were buried.

Emma Savage (9)
Leighton Primary School, Orton Malborne

The Sun

The sun is a fiery gas sphere
Watching over the planets
It is a special star
Floating on a black sea
It is a king
Looking after the planets
The sun is like a golden crown
Ready to send his message
To the planets
It is like a light bulb in a lamp
Glowing in the blue sky.

Billie-Kate Ridlington (9)
Leighton Primary School, Orton Malborne

Pyramids

Layers and layers of limestone stones
Stretching up high to the twinkling stars
There for over 3000 years
Sandy stones gazing way above
An ancient pyramid
Towering over the desert
Lots of mysterious passages
Hiding the pharaoh's tombs
An incredible treasure
Undisturbed for centuries
Glimmering at sunset
Everyone stars in amazement
At the wonderful pyramids.

Michael Richardson (9)
Leighton Primary School, Orton Malborne

Incredible Egypt

An enormous tower
Reaching for the sky
As the golden blocks
Twinkle in the scorching sun
Long confusing passages
Hiding the pharaoh's chamber
The sandy pyramids

The never-ending blue cloth
Gently rippling to the Mediterranean
White-sailed feluccas
Travel up and down
Feeding the land
With the yearly floods
The shimmering Nile.

Shannon Stones (9)
Leighton Primary School, Orton Malborne

Boudicca

Queen of the Iceni
Long red hair
Tall and thin
Angry face
Fierce eyes
Harsh voice
Fought the Romans
With her sword and shield
Upset when the Romans
Killed her people
Drank poison
And died.

Bethany Gunn (8)
Leighton Primary School, Orton Malborne

Those Tears Of Pain

Tears of pain pour out of those eyes,
When they think of the shouting and lies.
Tears of pain run down that face,
Nothing could make this a better place.
No stupid poem
Could fix this home.
They would read it every day,
All things bad,
Just make them sad
In every single way.
Tears of pain pour out of those eyes,
When they think of the shouting and lies.
Tears of pain run down that face,
Nothing could make this a better place.

Alice Chapman (11)
Leighton Primary School, Orton Malborne

Bigger Than A Man

Scary woman
With long red hair
Lovely gold bracelets
A necklace round her neck
Evil
Bigger than a man
Fought the Romans
Drank poison
The queen of the Iceni,
Boudicca.

Marc Pummell (9)
Leighton Primary School, Orton Malborne

Tutankhamun

A trembling hand.
An anxious look.
An outstanding wait.
A greedy look.
A small hole.
A golden statue.
A deep dull distance.
A quivering worker.
A broken door.
An ordinary look.
A musty smell.
A vibrating hand.
A tomb of treasures.
A treasure cave.

Charlie Stretch (9)
Leighton Primary School, Orton Malborne

Queen Boudicca

Long red hair,
touching her hips.
Fierce brown eyes
stare from
her bloodthirsty face.
A tall powerful leader,
who inspired
the Celts to fight.
Riding in her cart,
a sword and shield
in her terrifying hands.
Boudicca, queen of the Iceni.

Kyle Johns (9)
Leighton Primary School, Orton Malborne

The Sun

The sun is a fiery coin
sending messengers around
the solar system.
Every time an enemy comes near
the sun rages
sending out masses
of flames and gas.
The king of the solar system
looks at his endless kingdom.

Catrina Rose (8)
Leighton Primary School, Orton Malborne

Mummy

M emories of years ago
U nderworlds you will never know
M ummies have rotted as years have passed
M ummies sometimes never last
Y ears and years ago, memories you will always know.

Carla Johnston & Georgina Richardson (8)
Leighton Primary School, Orton Malborne

Pyramids

P haraohs buried in pyramids
Y ellowing in the sun
R esolving
A ncient secrets
M emories of ancient times
I nteresting stories
D iamonds and gold in tombs
S everal treasures buried in the sand.

Daniela Zheleva
Leighton Primary School, Orton Malborne

Fairground Fun!

I'm going to the fairground to have some *fun!*
Going on the rides and eating a burger in a bun

First let's go on the ghost train and scream and shriek,
When we get to the end, I take a quick peek.

Let's go on the helter-skelter and slip and slide,
Here I go, whizzing down, what a ride!

Next, we go on the big wheel, what a view,
The only problem is the tremendous queue!

Now we go on the roller coaster, put your hands in the air,
When you get off, you have extremely messy hair!

Time to go on the dodgems, dodge in and out,
When someone bangs into you, you let out a shout.

Finally we go home from a very fun day,
It was worth coming here - even if we had to pay!

Louise Hooper (11)
Leighton Primary School, Orton Malborne

Boudicca

Long red hair
Down to her hips
Thick gold necklace
Round her neck
Colourful cloak
Round her shoulders
Sword and shield
In her hands
Fierce and terrifying
Queen of the Iceni.

Samantha D'Santos (9)
Leighton Primary School, Orton Malborne

Tutankhamun

A beating heart
A shivering hand
An exciting moment
A small hole
A creaking door
A scary mystery
A musty smell
An elegant statue
A dark room
A glowing candle
A squeaking rat
A dripping goo
A speechless man
A golden bed
An enchanting place.

Nicole Raven (8)
Leighton Primary School, Orton Malborne

The Sun

Like the pharaoh
Rules over the solar system
Watching his slaves
As they protect him
From the sun's asteroids
Sunspot eyes everywhere
Looking down at the slaves
Gigantic flames destroying
His enemies
Never, ever sleep
Always on guard.

Joshua Bishop (8)
Leighton Primary School, Orton Malborne

The Sun

Fiery red ball
Of the solar system
Keeping every planet
His servant
Throwing out fireballs
To all his enemies
Jupiter watching him
With its red eye on the sun
All the other planets
Spin round him
Trying to obey him
Knowing the enemies
Are going to attack
The sun helps to keep
Everyone safe.

Farheen Khan (9)
Leighton Primary School, Orton Malborne

Pompeii

One sunny day
It was rumbling
Suddenly, *bang!*
It exploded
In a stroke
Ash falling
Dust blowing
People choking
It's dark
Pompeii buried
Dead.

Stephen Brader (8)
Leighton Primary School, Orton Malborne

Guilt, Truth, Lies, Betrayal

Guilt, truth, lies, betrayal,
Thunder, rain, screams and hail,
Death, life, God and the Devil,
The world crashing down,
They can't hear the sound
Of them screaming,
Not believing
In such a horrid place,
Packing a large suitcase,
Ready for death, lies and betrayal,
Thunder, rain, screams and hail.

Victoria Cartledge (10)
Leighton Primary School, Orton Malborne

Mummy

M any thousands of years ago
U nder the sand
M ummies lying
M elting flesh on bones
Y uck!

Sam Harding (9)
Leighton Primary School, Orton Malborne

Mummies

M any thousands of years ago
U nderneath the golden sand
M ummies were wrapped up
M ysteries archaeologists solve
I nside a sarcophagus
E mbalmers wrapped them up
S ome body parts were stolen.

Dion Sembie-Ferris (9)
Leighton Primary School, Orton Malborne

Pyramids

P haraohs ruled the land of Egypt.
Y ellow, hot sun shining down to the pyramids.
R ising mummies from the dead.
A mazing tomb paintings on the wall.
M any mummies were created.
I nteresting gold in the pharaoh's tomb.
D igging for treasure.
S ecret treasure buried under sand.

Rahib Alumia (9)
Leighton Primary School, Orton Malborne

Tutankhamun

Fandabbydocious archaeologist.
A thundering heart.
An amazing discovery.
A tomb of light.
A musty smell.
A smell of dripping perfumes.
An ancient tomb.
An open door.
Some shining gold.

Kyle Eldred (9)
Leighton Primary School, Orton Malborne

Pyramid

P eople dying
Y ears ago
R iver Nile flowing
A pharaoh's tomb
M emories are lost slowly
I n the rough wind
D ark tunnels everywhere.

Emma Bennetto (8)
Leighton Primary School, Orton Malborne

Tutankhamun

A tomb of life
A dark hole
A mystery to solve
A myth to find
A golden present
A scattering of jewellery
An ancient door
A speechless man
A vibrating hand
An amazing gold case
A huge tunnel
A beautiful sight
A thundering heart
An old king
A magical moment.

Rebecca Lancaster & Shannon (9)
Leighton Primary School, Orton Malborne

Tutankhamun

A gold case
An anxious wait
A satisfying animal
A sparkle of treasure
A shining torch
A glamorous place
A mercy smell
A weird tomb
A low-pitched voice
A wail of excitement.

Ryan Toner & Shenna (9)
Leighton Primary School, Orton Malborne

Tutankhamun

A trembling hand
An anxious wait
A tiny hole
A nervous archaeologist
An ebony tomb
A flickering candle
A shining torch
A smell of musty floors
A whiff of perfume
A distance of glittering gold
A speechless man
A discovery to be made
An explorer in the tomb.

Sarah Kingston (9) & Jadine Howlett (8)
Leighton Primary School, Orton Malborne

Tutankhamun

A pair of trembling hands.
Two knocking knees.
A small hole.
A lot of servants muttering.
The gold shining.
An anxious wait.
A strong smell of perfume.
A flickering candle.
An amazing discovery.
An amazing sight.
A treasured secret.

Shekinah Parrish (7)
Leighton Primary School, Orton Malborne

River Nile

A beautiful bend
A curved wave
A stunning source of water
A lovely blue colour
A large busy place
A lovely place to be.

Emma King & Shannon Curley (8)
Leighton Primary School, Orton Malborne

Tutankhamun

A hole in the wall
A candle shining in the darkness
A musty smell lingering in the air
A speechless person
An impatient crowd crowded around
A heart beating fast in someone's body
A treasure hidden in the tomb
A glint of gold
An amazing find.

Julie Watkin (9)
Leighton Primary School, Orton Malborne

River Nile

River
A great river
A gurgling river
A bump and a bend
An Egyptian paradise.

Matthew Hawes (9)
Leighton Primary School, Orton Malborne

Tutankhamun!

A trembling hand
A small hole
A pounding heart
A dusty door
A mountain of glaring gold
A musty smell
A lingering perfume
A shadow of past statues
A whispering whisper
A speechless voice
A pile of rubble
A fantastic sight
A row of elegant statues
A sparkling candle
A rich and happy life
A mystery to be solved.

Shannon Curley & Emma Savage (9)
Leighton Primary School, Orton Malborne

Tutankhamun

A tiny whisper
A trembling hand
A golden surprise
An animal statue
A horrid smell
An enormous wait
A strong smell
A golden sight
A mighty cry.

Tyler Nicholls & Kelsey Duberry (8)
Leighton Primary School, Orton Malborne

The River Nile

The soft gentle river
Floating in the breeze
People getting drinks
Playing in the river
Having so much fun
The river brings love and happiness to everyone.

Daniel Ward & Shekinah Parrish (8)
Leighton Primary School, Orton Malborne

Sadness

Sadness is like an annoying sound
Bumping through your ears.
Sadness feels like you have just been
Taken and nobody cares about you.
Sadness tastes like all of your mouth
Has gone dry and sour.
Sadness smells like a bonfire has just
Blown up in front of your face
And all your stuff's gone with it!

Charlotte Kerr (10)
Manea Community School, Manea

Darkness

Darkness is the colour of a black sky
It smells like black dust
It looks like the night
It feels scary
It reminds me of something nasty
It sounds like the wind.

Daniel McDermott (9)
Manea Community School, Manea

Love

Love is flowers and nice gestures.
Love is a twinkling of your eye that someone sees.
Love is a heart beating slowly with signs you've never seen.
Love is the flame of a candle.
Love is the words 'I love you'.
Love is the first kiss.

Jamie Francis (11)
Manea Community School, Manea

Fear

When you come face to face with it
You can hear your heart pounding like a drum inside you.
You can automatically smell fear from a mile away.
The foul taste you get when fear is near.
When the light goes out, you get one scary cold shiver
That slithers straight down your spine and you can't sleep.
Fear, you can't see it in our world
But you can see it in your mind.
Fear is the feeling of worry you have when you think
You are in danger or that something bad might happen.
When fear hits you, it rattles your brain,
Like someone is pushing and pulling you.

Ashley Bridgement (9)
Manea Community School, Manea

Love

L ove is the colour of very bright purple lavender
O range, oranges are the lovely smells of love
V iolets have the look of love and it feels like lovely
    smooth violets in your hand
E motion is part of love.

Stevie Harrow (8)
Manea Community School, Manea

War!

Smash! Boom!
I can hear
Horrible, deafening sounds,
Bombshells dropping nearby,
I'm closing my eyes.

I can smell
Sickening smells,
Gun resin,
Freshly killed and decaying bodies.

I can taste
Revolting
Air and smoke,
Feeling horrible.

I open my eyes,
It is devastating.
Exploded vehicles,
Hundreds maybe thousands of
Dead people.

The floor is covered in dead bodies,
Walking over them,
They crunch as I walk,
Bones and glass.

Dan Sansom (11)
Manea Community School, Manea

Fun

Fun is like the blue sky.
It smells like a flower.
It looks like a cloud.
It reminds me of the sea.

Callum Baker (10)
Manea Community School, Manea

Fun

Purple is the colour of fun
Fun smells like a bunch of flowers on a sunny day
Fun feels like a big fluffy cloud in a blue sky
It reminds me of something I have done in the past.

Asia Fox (9)
Manea Community School, Manea

Feelings

Some feelings are bad.
Some feelings are sad.
Some feelings are good.
Some feelings are happy.
Good feelings make you feel happy inside.
Bad feelings make you feel upset and sad,
That makes you feel you are not very good at anything.
My feelings today are happy.
Being happy feels warm and free.
When my feelings are hurt, it makes me feel sad.
Feelings are precious, they are nice to have.
Feelings are quiet and smooth.

Sarah Day (11)
Manea Community School, Manea

Love

L ove is like a river of red flowing around,
Sensing a smell of flowers.
O verflowing, reminding me of my heart.

V iolence has gone away.
I get the feeling of freedom.
E verybody is talking softly around me.

Kelly Howell (9)
Manea Community School, Manea

Silence

Silence is as clear and blank as a piece of paper.
Silence is like a bare world with nothing in it.
Silence feels like a television on mute.
Silence is when a leaf drops from its oak tree.
Silence gives you frustration in your veins.

Jake Winter (9)
Manea Community School, Manea

Poem Of Happiness

Happiness is when I'm playing with my friends.
Happiness is when I'm eating ice creams
And swimming in my swimming pool on a hot day.
Happiness is for when I'm riding my horse in a windy gallop.
Happiness is for when I have cool parties or discos.
Happiness is for when I go shopping and I buy loads of cool stuff
With my pocket money.
Happiness is for when I go to school to learn things
And see all my friends.
Happiness is for when I'm riding my bike to my friend's house.

Louisha Connolly (11)
Manea Community School, Manea

Anger

Anger is the colour of red, juicy meat dripping with dark red blood.
It smells like a lion about to pounce that makes me shiver and quiver.
Anger looks like a very angry dog about to tuck into fresh meat.
Anger feels like a tiger ripping through your skin.
Anger reminds me of two lions fighting.

Caitlin Wilby (9)
Manea Community School, Manea

Hate

Hate is the colour of red like a thorn bush.
It smells like fear in someone's eyes.
It looks like a coward afraid to tell the truth.
It feels as though a volcano has just erupted inside of you.

Conner Howell (9)
Manea Community School, Manea

Hunger

As I wander the deserted streets I gaze at
The wafting smells of baked bread.
A sudden whiff of delicious food passes by
While my tummy shrivels up.
The taste in my dry mouth is ravenous
And bitter while my jaw drops open with hunger.
When I roam past all of the cookery shops
I hear the noise of my belly rumbling as it shrinks.
I feel as if my ribs are breaking because
I feel so empty and skinny.

Leanne Spry (11)
Manea Community School, Manea

Sadness

Sadness makes me feel black,
When I'm sad I cry a waterfall,
I feel lost in my whole body,
It smells like damp air,
It reminds me of my old dog.

Kieran Howell (9)
Manea Community School, Manea

Fear

Fear is a feeling that I don't like,
With just a smell of black smoke,
I feel cold when I meet my fear,
I have chills running up and down my spine.

As I stand still,
With my feet glued to the ground,
I hear a murmur in my brain,
I feel dead.

Walking through the street,
Silence has been spread everywhere,
I have the taste of a sour peppermint in my mouth,
My head is dark and blank.

Sharon Howell (11)
Manea Community School, Manea

Silence

Silence is like the night,
Soundless as a mouse.

Silence is like empty space,
In a topsy-turvy world.

Silence can taste bitter,
Fiery and hot.

Silence feels like danger,
Just waiting for you.

Silence feels like white smoke,
Just waiting to surround you.

Silence is like
The first crack of dawn.

Suzanne Larham (11)
Manea Community School, Manea

Anger

Anger is like a bomb that can explode at any time.
Anger is the strongest feeling.
Anger is like a devil has taken over your body.
It sounds like a bomb is about to explode inside your head.
The best way to stop anger is to stop what you're doing
And count to ten.

Jack Lilley (11)
Manea Community School, Manea

Angry

Angry is like a roaring, thundering, gigantic tornado.
Angry feels too hot to touch, so mind you don't get burnt.
Angry tastes so bitter and soapy.
Angry smells like hot candle wax burning.
Angry looks like an orange thundering tornado.
Angry reminds me of an angry volcano.
Most people get angry because of annoying things.

Georgina Fitzgibbon (10)
Manea Community School, Manea

Darkness

D anger in the frightening dark
A shiver ran down my spine
R unning from the dooming darkness
K icking away from the scent of fear
N ow it feels like the Earth is empty
E ntering my garden, I look back at the dull sky
S ounds like the world is empty, no trees, no animals, no one
S o, as I taste the air, it is tasteless.

Jaimee-Leigh Webb (10)
Manea Community School, Manea

Anger

Anger is fierce like a volcano spitting out lava,
It never smells nice, it is just like a dragon breathing fire and smoke,
It smells like a gas bomb that has just gone off,
It sounds like a train coming towards you,
It looks like a demon destroying the world with his red hands.

Nikki Hopkin (10)
Manea Community School, Manea

Fear!

Fear sounds like a klaxon at a football ground.
Fear tastes as dry as the driest desert in the world
And all there is to wash it out is the dirtiest water known to man.
Fear smells like an endless dump taking over the world
Formed by a monster eating anything in its way
And there's no way out.
Fear looks like an endless pit and me just falling and falling!
Fear feels as sharp as a shark's tooth biting on a helpless fish.

George Burton (10)
Manea Community School, Manea

Silence

Silence is like everything has come to its death.
Nothing moves.
All you can feel is a *gust* of wind.
It feels as if everywhere has turned into a ghost town.
Silence looks like a new ice age is coming.
Everything has died.

Daniel Davies (11)
Manea Community School, Manea

Happiness

Happiness is the colour of pink and yellow.
It smells like flowers on a summer's day.
Happiness reminds me of my friends and family.
It makes me feel happy.

Kate Baxter (9)
Manea Community School, Manea

War!

Smash! Bang!
I nearly got deafened by the fierce crashing
Of a bombshell hitting the ground.
I had to cover my nose because of the revolting smell of smoke,
Burning vehicles and rotting bodies.
I am beginning to get a sore throat
As the burning smell of smoke slides past my tonsils
And down into my lungs.
The firing that the soldiers are shooting
Sounds like loud falling of hail.
I am hiding behind the remains of a blown-up truck
Hoping and praying that it is all a dream.

George McCarthy (11)
Manea Community School, Manea

Happiness

Happiness is like a summer's day.
With families and friends with cheer.
With hearts and flowers around.
Then the smell of sweet daisies and roses.
The colour of a smile is happiness.

Shanice Setchfield (10)
Manea Community School, Manea

Anger

Anger is the colour of blood.
It smells like sweat.
It looks like the veins are going to burst.
Anger, you feel like you are going to kill yourself.
Anger reminds me of when my dad died.

Adam Fenn (9)
Manea Community School, Manea

Fear

A soldier is like being a prisoner
In the middle of a life or death situation.
Fear tastes like air full of smoke
That just wants to make you choke.
Fear feels as though your life has just
Been taken out of your body.
Fear sounds like machine guns
Pounding on the ground and shooting people dead.
It looks like struggling soldiers trying
To find shelter.
Fear smells like rats and sewers
Leaking through the disgusting ground.

Darcy Attrill (10)
Manea Community School, Manea

Darkness

The colour black is like the night sky.
Darkness smells really dusty.
It looks like it's going to rain.
It feels like it's going to rain hard.
I was scared when it was raining.

Ashley Bullman (8)
Manea Community School, Manea

Love

Love is like a heart beating.
My friend in adoration at me,
Her devoted friend.
Love is as quiet as a fly
Landing on the work surface.
Love is the scent of a rose
In the middle of a romantic meal.

Courtney Milner (11)
Manea Community School, Manea

Happiness

Happiness is when I play with my friends.
Singing and dancing and playing fun games.
Eating ice cream on a nice hot day.
Playing at the park with some of my friends.
Happiness is when I eat my ice cream
Watching the wet, melting cream.

Rebecca Lawrence (10)
Manea Community School, Manea

Anger

Anger is red like a firing volcano.
It smells of a tasty, juicy cherry.
It feels like water running down my hands.
It reminds me of a red, silky, watery river.
It looks like red blood running down from my body.

Abbie Burridge (10)
Manea Community School, Manea

Darkness

Darkness is a sign of danger coming towards you.
It smells like something bad is going to happen.
Darkness looks like a night sky with danger floating around in it.
It feels like danger near me.
It reminds me of getting killed.

Ryan Spry (9)
Manea Community School, Manea

I'd Rather Be . . .

I'd rather be a horse than hay
I'd rather night than day

I'd rather be a mum than a dad
I'd rather be happy than sad

I'd rather be rich than poor
I'd rather be a window than a door

I'd rather be a cat than a dog
I'd rather be a rat than a frog

I'd rather be shoes than socks
I'd rather be keys than locks

I'd rather be children than toys
I'd rather be girls than boys

I'd rather be a word than a letter
I'd rather be worse than better

I'd rather be lemons than lime
I'd rather be oranges than wine

I'd rather be Ant than Dec
I'd rather be a body than a neck

I'd rather be onion than cheese
I'd rather be thank you than please.

Naomi Adams (10)
Middlefield CP School, Eynesbury

I'd Rather Be . . .

I'd rather be Barbie than Ken,
I'd rather be Bill than Ben.
I'd rather be a queen than a king,
I'd rather be a necklace than a ring.

I'd rather be Mum than Dad,
I'd rather be good than bad.
I'd rather be biscuits than tea,
I'd rather be a leg than a knee.

I'd rather be fat than thin,
I'd rather be rubbish than a bin.
I'd rather be Ant than Dec,
I'd rather be Donkey than Shrek.

I'd rather be conditioner than shampoo,
I'd rather be a panda than bamboo.
I'd rather be fish than chips,
I'd rather be Doritos than dips.

I'd rather be Nipper than Gnasher,
I'd rather be Blitzen than Dasher.

Daniella Chapman (9)
Middlefield CP School, Eynesbury

I'd Rather Be . . .

I'd rather be needle than thread
I'd rather alive than dead

I'd rather be a robber than a cop
I'd rather be a bucket than a mop

I'd rather be a fin than a tail
I'd rather be a hammer than a nail

I'd rather be a dog than a cat
I'd rather be skinny than fat

I'd rather be the moon than the sun
I'd rather be Dad than Mum.

Brady Mayes (11)
Middlefield CP School, Eynesbury

I'd Rather Be . . .

I'd rather be Ant than Dec,
I'd rather be a body than a neck,
I'd rather be Minnie than Mickey,
I'd rather be easy than tricky,
I'd rather be biscuits than tea,
I'd rather be legs than a knee,
I'd rather be ice cream than jelly,
I'd rather be clean than smelly,
I'd rather be Tom than Jerry,
I'd rather be a bush than a berry,
I'd rather be a moon than a sun,
I'd rather be icing than a bun,
I'd rather be vinegar than salt,
I'd rather be a door than a bolt,
I'd rather be a horse than a pony,
I'd rather be soap than foamy,
I'd rather be children than toys,
I'd rather be girls than boys.

Rebecca Riley-Brown (9)
Middlefield CP School, Eynesbury

I'd Rather Be . . .

I'd rather be on than off
I'd rather be a sneeze than a cough

I'd rather be bangers than mash
I'd rather be a smash than a crash

I'd rather be Spongebob than Patrick
I'd rather be wires than electric

I'd rather be Donkey than Shrek
I'd rather be Ant than Dec

I'd rather be a sister than a brother
I'd rather be a father than a mother.

Peter Moore (10)
Middlefield CP School, Eynesbury

Things That Puzzle Me

There are a few things in life that puzzle me
And here are just a few . . .

You can go to a rock concert
But don't get crushed.

You can enter a bar
But mind your head.

You could be cool
But you might get too cold.

You can eat a pike
But be careful of the spike.

You could be called Nick
But you might get arrested.

You can stand on Earth
But make sure it's dry.

There are a few things in life that puzzle me.

Luke Deakin (10)
Middlefield CP School, Eynesbury

Things That Puzzle Me

There are some things in life that puzzle me
And here are just a few . . .

You can work out the mean of anything you want,
But people won't be friends with you anymore.

You can catch a fly but it can't help you to go in the sky.

You can cross the road but make sure you calm down afterwards.

You can sear glass but be careful it doesn't cut you.

You can pick up a box but be sure that you don't get a punch by it.

There are things in life that puzzle me.

Katie Lei (10)
Middlefield CP School, Eynesbury

I'd Rather Be . . .

I'd rather be young than old
I'd rather be silver than gold

I'd rather be a knife than a fork
I'd rather be pudding than pork

I'd rather be Chip than Dale
I'd rather be brown than pale

I'd rather be on than off
I'd rather sniff than cough

I'd rather be a princess than a prince
I'd rather be beef than mince

I'd rather be Donkey than Shrek
I'd rather be Ant than Dec

I'd rather be a tree than leaves
I'd rather be a car than keys.

Liam Irons (9)
Middlefield CP School, Eynesbury

I'd Rather Be . . .

I'd rather be Paul than Barry
I'd rather be Minty than Garry

I'd rather be a wasp than a bee
I'd rather be coffee than tea

I'd rather be on than off
I'd rather be a skater than a goff

I'd rather be a dog than a cat
I'd rather be an owl than a bat

I'd rather be chips than pizza
I'd rather be a fridge than a freezer

I'd rather be a window than a door
I'd rather be rich than poor.

George Gifford (10)
Middlefield CP School, Eynesbury

Things That Puzzle Me

There are some things in life that puzzle me
And here are just a few . . .

You can take your bird to the bar
But make sure she doesn't fly away.

You can open the blind
But you still won't be able to see.

You can pick up a box
But make sure it doesn't punch.

You can sleep in a bed
But you always wake up the flowers.

You can eat a chip
But the computer won't work anymore.

You can catch a fly
But it won't take you to France.

You can fiddle with a pencil
But it won't play any music.

Kieran Singh Dale (10)
Middlefield CP School, Eynesbury

I'd Rather Be . . .

I'd rather be a biscuit than tea.
I'd rather be you than me.

I'd rather then small than tall.
I'd rather be cool than cruel.

I'd rather be happy than sad.
I'd rather be good than bad.

I'd rather be a horse than a pony.
I'd rather be bony than moany.

I'd rather be Billy than silly.
I'd rather be Minnie than Mickey.

Anna Higham (9)
Middlefield CP School, Eynesbury

I'd Rather Be . . .

I'd rather be Perry than Kevin
I'd rather be Hell than Heaven

I'd rather be a tiger than a lion
I'd rather be a board than an iron

I'd rather be Mum than Dad
I'd rather be happy than sad

I'd rather be Spongebob than Patrick
I'd rather be wires than electric

I'd rather be A than B
I'd rather be he than she

I'd rather be Tom than Jerry
I'd rather be a bush than a berry.

Josh Davis (10)
Middlefield CP School, Eynesbury

I'd Rather Be . . .

I'd rather be Kevin than Perry.
I'd rather be Tom than Jerry.

I'd rather be a doctor than a nurse.
I'd rather be a wallet than a purse.

I'd rather be the sun than the moon.
I'd rather be a fork than a spoon.

I'd rather be Jack than Jill.
I'd rather be a mountain than a hill.

I'd rather be Mum than Dad.
I'd rather be happy than sad.

Andrew Cate (11)
Middlefield CP School, Eynesbury

Things In Life Puzzle Me

There are things in life that puzzle me
And here are just a few . . .

You can fiddle with a pencil in your hand
But it might start to make music

You can point to someone
But be careful it's not too sharp

You can kick a ball
But it might start to dance

You can swallow
But you might start singing

You can listen to rock
But it won't make a sound

You can cross the road
But make sure you calm down afterwards

You can hog a bike
But it might bite you

You need space
But be careful you don't float away

You can chip a plate
But please don't eat it

There are things in life that puzzle me.

Josie Hayter (10)
Middlefield CP School, Eynesbury

I'd Rather Be . . .

I'd rather be Ant than Dec
I'd rather be Donkey than Shrek

I'd rather be fat than thin
I'd rather be rubbish than a bin

I'd rather be fruit than veg
I'd rather be an arm than a leg

I'd rather be Mum than Dad
I'd rather be happy than sad

I'd rather be a sock than a foot
I'd rather be a trainer than a boot

I'd rather be Abel than Kane
I'd rather be Tarzan than Jane

I'd rather be nits than hairy
I'd rather be Pippin than Merry

I'd rather be Tom than Jerry
I'd rather be Kevin than Perry

I'd rather be she than he
I'd rather be you than me

I'd rather be young than old
I'd rather be hot than cold

I'd rather be a panda than bamboo
I'd rather be conditioner than shampoo

I'd rather be biscuits than tea
I'd rather be a leg than a knee.

Thomas Jenner (10)
Middlefield CP School, Eynesbury

I'd Rather Be . . .

I'd rather be Chip than Dale,
I'd rather be brown than pale.

I'd rather be Mum than Dad,
I'd rather be good than bad.

I'd rather be on than off,
I'd rather be a skater than a goff.

I'd rather be a rat than a mouse,
I'd rather be a cat than a house.

I'd rather be a sword than a shield,
I'd rather be a horse than a field.

I'd rather be a sock than a shoe,
I'd rather be me not you.

I'd rather be new than old,
I'd rather be cool than gold.

I'd rather be Bill than Ben,
I'd rather be women than men.

Shane McDonald (10)
Middlefield CP School, Eynesbury

Rugby

Red is for the concentration before a penalty or conversion.
Brown is for the wet mud.
Light and dark blue are for the St Neot's rugby colours.
Orange is for the joy after you've scored a try.
Green is for the few blades of grass left after a match.

Adam Williams (8)
Priory Junior School, St Neots

The Colour Of Feelings

Hunger
Is an empty purple, like violets on a sunny day.

Anger
Is a fiery red, like the sunshine on a boiling desert.

Jealousy
Is a leafy green, like the seaweed at the deepest part of the sea.

Fun
Is a bright orange, like the start of a roaring fire.

Sadness
Is a deep blue, like the bottom of a lake.

Laughter
Is a lovely yellow, like the rays of the sun.

Sally Barker (9)
Priory Junior School, St Neots

Colour

What colour is happiness?
It is yellow like the sun joyfully warming the Earth.

What colour is hunger?
It is brown like the earth in a famine.

What colour is anger?
It is red like lava spilling out of a volcano.

What colour is sleepiness?
It is white like a soft pillow.

What colour is excitement?
It is gold like treasure in a chest.

What colour is joy?
It is silver like tinsel on a Christmas tree.

Joe O'Connor (8)
Priory Junior School, St Neots

What Colour Is . . .

What colour is darkness?
Darkness is black like the silent night.
What colour is anger?
Anger is red like fresh-spilt blood.
What colour is happiness?
Happiness is green like healthy grass.
What colour is sunshine?
Sunshine is yellow like the great, golden sun.
What colour is silence?
It is grey like stone.
What colour is laughter?
It is blue like the deep oceans.
What colour is fear?
It is black like darkness.
What colour is jealousy?
It is red like a great fire.

Philip Hamilton (10)
Priory Junior School, St Neots

Emotions

Joy
Is for sweet flowers on Valentine's Day

Hope
Is for the lovely sunset at night

Love
Is for friendships and kindness to one another

Fear
Is for tiptoeing through forests and woods.

Emma Blacow (9)
Priory Junior School, St Neots

Colours Of Life

Darkness is black like the light being turned off at night.
Love is white like the constant stars above.
Happiness is gold like the sparkling sun in the blue, bird-filled sky.
Anger is dark orange like the flames of a raging fire.
Cosiness is red like the pumping of a loving heart.
Sadness is grey like a long winding road to nowhere.
Warmth is a mixture of yellow, orange and red like in the setting sun.
Boredom is painting something magnolia and watching it dry.
Life is made up of many shades of colours like those found in the
rainbow.

Mary Lundie (10)
Priory Junior School, St Neots

Fairy Of Horror

The fairy of horror frightens you head to toe
She kills the frogs in your pond
And the tadpoles to scare the birds
Whatever can we do?

Annie Harvey-Nash (7)
Priory Junior School, St Neots

Colours

Laughter is the sound of happy faces,
Silence is blue like the silent sky,
Hunger is red like your empty tummy,
Fun is green like 'go and play!'
Anger is the sound of deep, dark nights,
Sunshine is yellow like a sunflower,
Fear is the colour of gloomy green like the woods,
Sadness is a white background with no friends,
Moonlight is the shape of a smile,
Darkness is black with twinkling stars.

Megan Evans & Hayley Cameron (8)
Priory Junior School, St Neots

Playtime

P als
L itter picking
A rguing
Y elling
T elling
I gnoring
M iming
E veryone is having fun.

Elizabeth Jones (9)
St Augustine's Junior School, Peterborough

Lunchtime

L is for laughing out loud
U is for unwrapping my banana cake
N is for the nice dinner ladies
C is for the nice chairs that we sit on
H is for a hungry belly
T is for teaching a new game
I is for inviting people to play a game
M is for munching my food
E is for eating my one and only cake.

Rhian Jones (9)
St Augustine's Junior School, Peterborough

Playtime

P is for pulling at somebody's clothes
L is for laughing at each other's jokes
A is for arguing about something silly
Y is for yelling because it's fun
T is for throwing things very far
I is for identifying my friends
M is for muttering to my best friends
E is for everyone in the school.

Emily Dobbins-Houldridge (8)
St Augustine's Junior School, Peterborough

Playtime

P is for playing football
L is for laughing
A is for arguing with my friends
Y is for the yellow sunshine
T is for getting told off
I is for an ice pack
M is for my teacher shouting
E is for eating my biscuits.

Tyler Coddington (9)
St Augustine's Junior School, Peterborough

Playtime

P is for playing
L is for listening
A is for arguing
Y is for yelling
T is for throwing
I is for imagining
M is for muttering
E is for everyone.

Romina Vila (9)
St Augustine's Junior School, Peterborough

Playtime

P is for playing with your pals
L is for laughing and being loud
A is for arguing and getting angry
Y is for yelling and playing yo-yo
T is for training and playing tennis
I is for impressing the teacher and playing 'it'
M is for being mean and moaning
E is for the ending of playtime and everyone goes home.

Ella Broccoli (9)
St Augustine's Junior School, Peterborough

Playtime

P laytime is the best time in the world
L ying to my friends
A round the field I go,
Y elling across the playground
T easing and tigging
I ce pack on my head
M oaning and maths
E veryone is playing.

Sian Jones (9)
St Augustine's Junior School, Peterborough

Playtime

P is for pals amazing you
L is for laughing with your friends
A is for arguing with your enemies
Y is for yelling at people,
T is for throwing balls around,
I is for incredible games to play,
M is for being mad with your friends,
E is for everyone having *brilliant* fun!

Jessica Fraser (9)
St Augustine's Junior School, Peterborough

Playtime

P is for pals and playing,
L is for laughing and lying,
A is for arguing and acting,
Y is for yelling and little youngsters running,
T is for trim-trail and telling tales,
I is for incredible and invisible playtime
M is for muddy socks and mumbling
E is for everybody and playing with Emily.

P - L - A - Y - T - I - M - E!

Chloe Rockliffe (8)
St Augustine's Junior School, Peterborough

Playtime Poem

Assembly's finished
People pushing to get out the door.
Boys running to get a good place to play football,
Girls doing handstands on the field.
Year 3 telling tales to teacher,
Everyone laughing and screaming,
And teacher saying, 'I can't hear myself think,'
People running across the concrete, falling down.
The bell goes and they all moan, time for maths.
They're still screaming when they line up,
People saying, 'You've pushed in!'
The teacher opens the door,
We come in slowly
Playtime's over.

Aileen Crosbie (9)
St Augustine's Junior School, Peterborough

Playtime

Playtime is children like wild animals
Playtime is seeing children playing games
Playtime is telling jokes
Playtime is getting told off
Playtime is children giggling
Playtime is being bullied
Playtime is me chatting
Playtime is me smiling
Playtime is fantastic
I wish I can do it all day!

Laura Belding (9)
St Augustine's Junior School, Peterborough

Break Time

B is for bats and balls bouncing backwards
R is for running round like rats
E is for everyone enjoying exciting play
A is for adventure and angry arguing
K is for kick when the ball goes up

T is for tuck shop, it takes so much time
I is for incredible when the snow turns into ice
M is for mud because they get so mucky
E is for eating, because everyone eats.

Jade Baron (8)
St Augustine's Junior School, Peterborough

Death By Sandwiches

One day my sister ate so much she burst
I cried, 'It must have been the worst,
Sausages are so bad for you,'
I said as my mum exploded too.
My brother thought it was quite funny,
Until he glanced at his own tummy,
As I watched my brother start to swell,
He let out a frightful yell.
As I suppressed a piercing scream,
He said, 'I've eaten too much cream.'
As the waitress came over to help,
I let out an enormous yelp,
I realised . . . yes it's true,
I had eaten a sandwich too!
A death by sandwich had come at last,
And I exploded with an almighty blast.

Kimberley Beaumont (11)
St Catherine's Preparatory School, Cambridge

The Brat And Me

When all is well and doing fine,
My sister yells to me, *'That's mine!'*
I say, 'What's yours? You little brat.'
'My favourite cuddly toy kitty-cat!'

Then she sticks out her tongue, directly at me,
And if you think that's as mean as she can be,
She socks me - hard - right in the tummy!
I'm telling you, it isn't funny!

When it seems as if it can't get worse,
She breaks my stylish, hot, pink purse!
My teddy bear and books long gone
I could've hit her with a gong!

Finally, when my parents see
How vicious my little sister can be
They stick her face in a pie full of cream!
(Okay - not really, but in my dreams!)

So there you go, that's all for now,
You see my sis can give a *pow!*
So every day it's the same - you see,
It's me, and the brat, the brat and me!

Allie Tiger (11)
St Catherine's Preparatory School, Cambridge

The Weekends

Weekends the wonderful way to relax
Having fun with friends and cash!
Wandering and lurking in the crowd
Bumping into people you know around

A fresh cappuccino, inside, adults sit and chat
While we're standing outside in our wet and gungy rain macs!
Waiting at the bus stop to be collected
Arrived at the doorstep put my key in the lock
And there is my family looking at our new clock.

Sophie Rawe (11)
St Catherine's Preparatory School, Cambridge

Seasons

Springtime:-
Fresh dew sparkles on the grass
Bulbs open up
Flowers begin to bloom
Days begin to get longer.

Summer:-
Endless sunny days
Water fights all day
Fruit beginning to get ripe
Flowers in full bloom.

Autumn:-
Lots of ripe fruit ready to be eaten
Spending less time outside
Animals start to hibernate
Conkers galore.

Winter:-
Trees start to die
Frost freezes everything
Preparing for snow
And it's almost Christmas.

Nicola Taylor (10)
St Catherine's Preparatory School, Cambridge

When The Teacher Leaves The Room

When the teacher leaves her settled class.
The children leap into action,
Like toys awaking at night.
Rubbers soar across the room,
People duck to avoid them.
A pile of tatty coats is made,
Ready for people to leap on.
Suddenly the teacher moves the door,
The children leap into seats, as if they'd never stirred.

Jenny Kent (11)
St Catherine's Preparatory School, Cambridge

Witches

A witch cackles,
Her wand crackles,
Her broomstick soars,
Through the dark sky.

Alakazam!
Almighty bangs,
The witch she cries,
In almost delight.

The wolves they howl,
Twoo! Hoots the owl,
The witch trail sparks,
High across the sky.

No noise is there,
Anywhere,
The witch is home,
She is all alone.

Lucy Hitchcock (10)
St Catherine's Preparatory School, Cambridge

The Beach

Like a slithering snake,
Golden sand slips through fingers.
Then the tide comes, takes it back,
Away from those who linger.

Sandcastles are constructed and
The sand is dotted with shells.
Air is filled with sea salt,
And fabulous seaweed smells.

The emerald-green waves,
Crash onto the sandy shore.
Then sweep up pearl-white shells,
And are gone for evermore.

Joanna Leader (10)
St Catherine's Preparatory School, Cambridge

Galaxy

No, not the chocolate,
the place above us.
You know, the place that glimmers, shines,
In the night.

Astronomers watch through the lens of telescopes,
define certain stars and think deep thoughts.
I too am an astronomer,
I watch and think about my galaxy.

Every night,
through my skylight
I witness a jeweller's shop's display
On jet-black velvet.

I search for my gods
Castor and Pollux,
the Gemini,
always there to watch me, guide me, help me.

Cressida Rigney (11)
St Catherine's Preparatory School, Cambridge

The Woman Out Of The Mist

The moon glows as the woman steps out of the mist
and shows her colours of shimmering gold.
The girl walks her steady path home as the night begins to get cold.
The path turns and the mist of gold gets brighter
and the girl remembers what she has been told.
The light seems to go out, the cold and the mist seem to close in upon
the little girl as she passes the trees in mould.
The girl hears a song that leads her to the lake under the power she
cannot break, not ever remembering the story she had been told.
The girl lies in the water, her face white and cold.
The woman out of the mist sinks back into her grave, another
fifty years until she can show her colours of gold.

Emma Marriott (11)
St Catherine's Preparatory School, Cambridge

How The Cat

How the cat sunbathes on a roof of a car.
How the cat pounces on a pink mouse's tail.
How the cat sleeps like a hedgehog curled in a ball.
How the cat waits for its milk at the door.
How the cat sits on my lap purring with contentment.
How the cat licks me like a naughty kitten.
I love my cat.

Megan Gilligan (11)
St Catherine's Preparatory School, Cambridge

When Day's Gone And Night Falls

When day's gone and night falls the sunset horizon slowly dies
When the moon sparkles like the most amazing crystal in the world.
The stars brightly glimmer and glide across the pitch-black.
Earthy sky like Heaven on wings up so high.

Megan Parkins (11)
St Catherine's Preparatory School, Cambridge

Winter

Water drips down, bristly, green Christmas tree.
Icy, cold, thick, diamond-white snow.
Never lasting ice glass floor.
Trees dressed up in shimmering frost.
Everlasting lingering mist covering the mystical city.
Restless somersaulting, bouncing, springing hail.

Antonia Foster (11)
St Catherine's Preparatory School, Cambridge

A Night In The Woods

I heard the scream of a child,
I heard the howl of a wolf,
I turned around,
Nobody was there.

I heard a young bear cry,
I heard the screech of an owl,
I turned around,
Nobody was there.

I heard a cry of pain,
I heard someone falling,
I turned around,
Nobody was there.

I turned back round,
There was someone,
Lying in front of me,
Not me.

Alex Sutcliffe (11)
St Catherine's Preparatory School, Cambridge

Mayhem

M y world is hectic, frantic
A lways frightened
Y elling in despair
H ardly seeming to understand.
E very day,
M y world is *Mayhem!*

Kitty Underwood (11)
St Catherine's Preparatory School, Cambridge

Dawn

The dawn sun rises,
Over the fields of cadmium rape.
Turning the sky into a rage of colours,
Crimson, scarlet, chrome and gold.

Young rabbits sprint in the fields below,
With their ivory cottontails bobbing.
Munching on blades of emerald grass,
And triumphant moorland heather.

In nests so carefully made,
Sit squawking fledglings waiting to be fed.
High up in the oak trees,
Overlooking their parents in the fields below,
Searching for food.

This is what I see from my window at dawn.

Charlotte Jeanroy (11)
St Catherine's Preparatory School, Cambridge

Toffee

In my hand is a toffee,
I will unwrap the wrapper,
And I will chew it until
I get another one next week,
Sticky as a slug,
I want another one,
But I'm not allowed,
So Mum, get me one,
Right now!
Or I will get past you
And get one myself!

Timothy Castling (8)
Wendover CE Junior School, Wendover

Toffee

So chewy and brown,
You want more when you have licked it.
As shiny as silver
So light in my mouth.
You pick up the packet and start to open it.
Your eyes are so shiny then . . .
Yum-yum . . .

You eat it!

Orie Amadi (8)
Wendover CE Junior School, Wendover

Pizza

The burning pepperoni turns my mouth into an inferno,
The cheese melts just like ice,
The cheese is as stretchy as an elastic band,
The tomato is as red as an apple,
The base is as light as a piece of bread.

Jack Wells (8)
Wendover CE Junior School, Wendover

Pasta

The creamy sauce,
The mouth-watering taste,
The lumps of tasty ham,
The white sauce is as white as snow,
My mum always gives me lots,
And I suck it in like a piece of spaghetti.

Tom Bedwell (8)
Wendover CE Junior School, Wendover

Blue Mints

Mints are as smooth as a piece of white paper.
They taste of mint toothpaste.
They are as blue as the sky.
They are very hard and crunchy.

And as small as a spider.
There are 12 in a packet.
When I open them, they make such a racket
I suck the mint flavour and I think I'm in heaven.

I want to eat them every single day
I can't eat them every single day.
You can eat them once in a while
I think they're so tasty to eat.

But my sister thinks they're revolting.
They sparkle as the sunny sun.
They are the greatest mints I've ever had.
They're so talented and scrumptious!

Ella Wallis (8)
Wendover CE Junior School, Wendover

Victoria Sponge Cake

It's as soft as satin,
And it sticks to my teeth like toffee,
It melts in my mouth, and the foamy cream
Is as thick as jungle rain
The cherries on top act as guards
For this irresistible cake,
As though they never want to leave it - like me!
It slides down my throat, like it's a giant snake.
It tickles my tum as it melts.

'Give me another!'

Charlotte Atkins (8)
Wendover CE Junior School, Wendover

My Dog Sassy

My dog Sassy
Is beautiful and brown,
She is ever so shaggy,
She never lets me down.

My dog Sassy
Takes *me* for walks
She is ever so big,
I wish she could talk.

My dog Sassy
Is so very gentle
She loves squeezy balls
And when she plays, she's mental.

My dog Sassy
I love her so much,
She is the bestest dog in the world,
She's gorgeous and soft to touch.

Zoe Freeman (11)
Wendover CE Junior School, Wendover

Pizza

It's blazing hot, it makes me hot
It tickles in my tum.
It feels like a sweetie.
It's chewy as a sweet.
As floppy as a jelly.
As delicate as grass.
As light as a sausage.
As spicy as some chillis
As light as loads of sweets.

Robin Geddes (7)
Wendover CE Junior School, Wendover

Homer's Love Poem

I'm fat and I'm round
And I'm not that good-looking
I drink lots of beer
And eat loads of home cooking
I don't like to work
And love the TV
Why are you married to me?

I shout at the children
And kick at the dog
I don't like the neighbour
And I'm a real road hog.
You're lovely and smart
You're pretty and kind
If you ever went away
I'd go out of my mind!

D'oh Homer XXX

Samuel Pring (11)
Wendover CE Junior School, Wendover

Who Am I?

My first is in light, but not in dark,
My second is in squeak and so not bark,
My third is in don't and also in do,
My fourth is in pink but never in blue,
My fifth is in clay and also in hay,
My sixth is in far but also in near,
My seventh is in day and never in night,
And, if you should see me, I'll put up a fight!

Who am I?

Answer: Leopard.

Amy McKay (11)
Wendover CE Junior School, Wendover

School SATs

A blank piece of paper just waiting for you
When you wake up I'm as scared as you

A minute to go, I'll be so slow
I won't get the highest grade don't you know

I'm trying to think but I've run out of ink
So hopefully a pencil will do

I'm sure it won't matter as long as I try
At least the ink won't need to dry

English, maths, science, where do I start?
I wish it were more interesting, like art

They look so hard but I'll have a go
I could just do it, you never know!

Emma Donald (10)
Wendover CE Junior School, Wendover

Cardigan Granny

'Twas winter and the old fogies
Did rumba classes in the hall,
All bored were the poor young children
Left to lean against the wall.

Beware the cardigan granny
She knits all day and all the night,
She makes you wear her cardigans
But don't put up a fight.

'Twas winter and the old fogies
Did rumba classes in the hall,
All bored were the poor young children
Left to lean against the wall.

Sarah Patton (10)
Wendover CE Junior School, Wendover

At The Battle Of Flanders Field

I'm here to report to you what's going on,
In World War I,
It is no fun,
We all have a gun.

Bullets are flying,
Soldiers are dying,
Relatives are crying.

There's a bomb coming,
Bang!
It's as loud as thunder
We need to get going,
Before the nerve gas,
Kills us all,
Because we don't want to fall.

We're all on attack,
There's no going back,
We're dropping like flies,
Because we keep running on mines.

The Germans are coming, out of their trenches,
As fast as bullets.
I'm going to die,
So this is goodbye.

Alex McGowan (11)
Wendover CE Junior School, Wendover

Strawberry

Strawberry, you're red and sweet,
You're my favourite fruit to eat.
Nothing compares with your smell,
Trust me, I can tell.
You also feel very soft, and when I take a little bite,
I know you will be my favourite forever.

Kane Pril (11)
Wendover CE Junior School, Wendover

Season's Child

There were autumn moons when I was new,
Then winter came and up I grew.
I went to school and learnt to write,
I learnt to play, I learnt to fight.
I made great friends, enemies too,
I began to know which ones were true.
There were autumn moons when I was new,
Then winter came and up I grew.

The lovely, stunning spring is here,
And so it means that summer's near.
I'm getting big, healthy and tall,
I took my tests and passed them all.
I got good grades and went to uni.
Met a mate called Abigail Moony.
There were autumn moons when I was new,
Then winter came and up I grew.

Emily Davies-Hawes (10)
Wendover CE Junior School, Wendover

The Hungry Mouse

There was a little mouse,
Who found a sack of grain,
He took a little nibble,
And ran back home again.

He ran into his mouse hole,
And scurried off to bed.
Dreams of grain and cats and cheese,
Were whirling in his head.

He woke up the next morning,
As hungry as a bear.
He went to find the sack of grain,
But shock! It wasn't there!

Charlotte Grimsdale (11)
Wendover CE Junior School, Wendover

The Robin

Beyond the crops so fine,
And past the field of daisies,
Over the rickety bridge,
And through the village of mazes,
Lives the little red robin,
Sitting on his perch,
Amongst the leaves of the silver birch.
Now here's a question,
What is he thinking?
Maybe he wishes to be bold and bright,
Like summer and spring,
Where there're bugs to bite.
Or maybe to sleep both day and night,
Or to be not so afraid of the kites.
He might wish to be smart and clever,
Like the old owl with the chestnut feather.
Beyond the crops so fine,
And past the field of daisies,
Over the rickety bridge,
And through the village of mazes,
Lives the little red robin,
Sitting on his perch,
Amongst the leaves of the silver birch.
The little red robin,
The little red robin,
Such a mystery is he.

Alys Reed (9)
Wendover CE Junior School, Wendover

Dirt

The mountain bike sprayed squelchy mud up.
They skidded into the bend.
The crowd got sprayed, sprayed, sprayed with mud.
The flag was up round the bend.
But he shot off into the crowd.

Jack Williamson (9)
Wendover CE Junior School, Wendover

Spring

It's turned from winter into spring,
My senses have awoken,
My dreams of sun and wonderful things,
Have surely not been broken.

The sweet smell of grass wafts up my nose,
While the bright yellow sun dries all of my clothes,
The clear, blue sky glistens like sea,
And the butterflies fly all around me.

It's turned from winter into spring,
My senses have awoken,
My dreams of sun and wonderful things,
Have surely not been broken.

Flowers stand, striking their pose,
Lambs are born in the sun,
Flowers' scents flow up my nose,
See the lambs playing and having fun.

Spring is the best season of all,
With the flowers, sun and sky,
We've had winter where the leaves fall,
But now spring is nigh.

It's turned from winter into spring
My senses have awoken,
My dreams of sun and wonderful things,
Have surely not been broken.

Louisa Down (11)
Wendover CE Junior School, Wendover

Monkey

His fur waving in the breeze and glistening in the sun,
Swooping through the trees.
Running from the hunter's gun.
Dodging the jaguar prowling in the tree,
This could only be the one and only monkey.

Ellen Blackburn (10)
Wendover CE Junior School, Wendover

Dreams

One of my dreams has once come true,
And that was for me to write to you.
Samantha's dreams always come true,
She always dreams of feeling blue.

Sarah's dreams are always stupid,
She dreams of riding Cupid.
Louisa's dreams are even worse,
She wants her life to be cursed.

Becky's dream is to perform,
We all say *'great'* just to conform.
Beth's dream is only horses,
She dreams of riding round the courses.

Chloe's dream is that Man City win,
She dreams but all people say is *'dim'*.
Zoe's dream is *judo, judo,*
She dreams about Mr Rudeo.

So we all have dreams, big and small,
But we must stop dreaming in school!

Emily Hogg (11)
Wendover CE Junior School, Wendover

Laughter

It tastes like chocolate melting in your mouth.
It smells like the sweetest smelling lily.
It sounds like your heart beating a thousand beats per minute.
It looks like a baby's first ever smile.
It feels like your heart is smiling back at you . . .
Laughter really is the best in the entire world.

Lauren Halpin (11)
Wendover CE Junior School, Wendover

Lonely

When I'm lonely
I'm sad
When I'm with someone
I'm happy
But sometimes it's the other way round.

It's sadness
It's happiness
But sometimes it's
Just pure evil.

It's dark
It's light
It's horrible for me

I wonder, I wonder
What it might be like,
If I wasn't by myself.

Eleanor Fenner (10)
Wendover CE Junior School, Wendover

Fear

Fear is red like a dagger
Flying into your head.
No more blood flowing around your body,
It's as black as the Devil's heart.
He will take your soul,
The fear can taste forever!
Your thought like a haunted mansion,
Beware fear is just around the corner.

James Edmonds (11)
Wendover CE Junior School, Wendover

The Sea

The sea is like a starry night,
Like a blue, watery, crystal sight,
The flowing breeze runs through my hair,
But it's very cold air,
I like to see the last star in the sky,
But when I look up, it's very high.

Hayley Morgan (9)
Wendover CE Junior School, Wendover

The Sky

The sky is a bright sheet of blue
The clouds are puffed up pillows
The night is a black sheet of darkness
The stars are the twinkle of pins
The moon is a ball of creamy yellow
The sun is a red ball when it sets
The Earth is a planet full of life.

Elena Marris (10)
Wendover CE Junior School, Wendover

Water

The slow water bubbling,
Tossing and turning,
It trickles down the waterfall,
Then it gets faster and faster,
No more bubbling,
No more twisting and no more turning.

Georgie Wilton (9)
Wendover CE Junior School, Wendover

How To Turn Lewis Into A Pig

Lots of ingredients are what I've got,
A pint of slugs in the pot.
A beak of a stork, a fat man's belly,
This is how I'll make Lewis smelly.

At midnight I will make this pot,
And give it to Lewis while it's still hot.

I'll shrink his arms; I'll shrink his legs,
Using the powder I kept in kegs.
This will make him buck and kick,
And Lewis will think, it is a trick.

At midnight I will make this pot,
And give it to Lewis while it's still hot.

One set of horse hooves, two lion eyes,
This will give Lewis thick thighs.
This is the pot, I will make big,
To turn Lewis into a pig.

Josh Bailey (11)
Wendover CE Junior School, Wendover

Girl Called Rose

There was a girl called Rose,
Her mum said, 'Give us a pose.'
She knelt on her knees,
Flung back her fleas,
And that was the end of her pose.

Chloe Coggins (11)
Wendover CE Junior School, Wendover

The Turkey That Never Went Down In The Tummy!

Once there was a turkey,
That never went down in the tummy!
The butcher chased him down the street,
Until the running hurt his feet!

The hunter got out his shotgun,
He missed the shot,
And hit an unfortunate one.

The fisherman went after the turkey,
In the end he had to eat jerky!

The whole town went after his feet,
Only to realise they had been beat.

The turkey went to his wife and children,
And never went out again.

Rory Griffiths (10) & Faisal Khan (9)
Wendover CE Junior School, Wendover

Jealousy

Jealousy looks like liquid, boiling on a stove,
Bubbling, bubbling until it pours over the edge and scars you for life.

Jealousy tastes so bitter it makes your tongue throb and go numb.

Jealousy sounds like an ear-splitting scream,
Never-ending, it just keeps on going and going.

Jealousy smells like burning rubber,
The strong smell that lasts forever and ever.

Jealousy feels like the skin of a porcupine,
Pricking and stabbing you until you bleed, never-ending.

Jealousy is a black cloud of rage
Towering over you, and slowly drowning you in darkness . . .

Rebecca McCleary (11)
Wendover CE Junior School, Wendover

The Haunted House

T antrum everywhere,
H ating noises,
E nchanted mysteries.

H orrendous ghost noises
A nonymous ghosts
U nwanted creaks of floorboards
N atural sound never found there,
T antrums are coming to you,
E xciting for no one,
D ead bodies everywhere.

H igh-pitched noises,
O ctagon-shaped carpets on the floors,
U npainted pictures on their walls,
S agging wallpaper
E clipse of the moon every day.

The name of this house is Haunted!

Helen Dawson (10)
Wendover CE Junior School, Wendover

Jerry And Ceri

There was a young girl called Ceri,
Who ate a big fat berry,
She walked along,
Singing her song,
And then met a boy called Jerry!

There was a boy called Jerry,
Who seemed very merry,
He drank a drink,
From the sink,
And met a girl called Ceri!

Zack Saunders (10)
Wendover CE Junior School, Wendover

The Newcastle Stars

Alan Shearer is his name,
Football is his game,
Passing to Dyer,
Cos his pants are on fire,
Playing the beautiful game.

Alan Shearer is his name,
Football is his game,
The cross is from Carr,
Hoorah! Hoorah!
Cos Shearer scored again.

Stephan Carr is his name,
Football is his game,
Always crossing for his teammates,
And dribbling past the players he hates,
Playing the beautiful game.

Stephan Carr is his name,
Football is his game,
Getting the ball from Dyer,
Although he is not dire,
Playing the beautiful game.

Kieron Dyer is his name,
Football is his game,
He plays in midfield,
And goals he yields,
Playing the beautiful game.

Kieron Dyer is his name,
Football is his game,
He's as fast as a rocket,
Cos there's speed in his pocket,
Playing the beautiful game.

Calum Findlay & Brett Collings (10)
Wendover CE Junior School, Wendover

Waterfall

Starting slowly in a stream,
Meandering slowly,
Eagerly growing into a river
Faster, faster,
Zooming, booming,
Crashing, crashing, bashing, gnashing,
Turning, gurgling, churning,
Going down, down,
A waterfall
Zooming, booming,
Meandering,
Slower, slower, soothing, relaxing.
Going back into a stream
Trickling slowly,
Eventually reaching the sea.

Shannon Skidmore (8)
Wendover CE Junior School, Wendover

Little Terrors

Bob is playing football,
Bert has got a gun.
Fred attempts to climb the wall,
Lucy's having fun.

James is eating chocolate,
Sam is climbing trees,
Amy's running round and round,
Robin's eating peas.

Teacher comes out,
Teacher goes back in,
What a lot of noise,
What a lot of din!

Jason Gooderham (10)
Wendover CE Junior School, Wendover

The Isle Of Plimp

On the Isle of Plimp
Where the Bong trees grow,
And brooks of liquorice water flow,
The very gentle plimpish breeze
Often carries little bees
Who cannot pay their debts in money
So they have to pay their debts in honey.

I once went there with a crew of pirates
Who called themselves the fly Emirates,
I once went there with a band of smugglers
Who were entertained by jolly jugglers
There are trusty badgers playing dice
With all the carol-singing mice.
Plimp contains some very strange plants,
If you saw them you'd think you were in a trance,
There's the dandelion that roars
And the poppy-cock that crows and caws.
It's the strangest place I've ever seen
And the Isle of Plimp is my dreamland.

Joseph Hodson (9)
Wendover CE Junior School, Wendover

Football

F ootball is fabulous
O range scarves flooding the stands
O xford ready to play
T ranmere revving up their gears
B all flies towards the goal
A way fans stand up and cheer as the ball smashes into the goal
L ong awaited full-time comes
'L osers,' shout the Oxford fans to the Tranmere players.

Ben Geddes (10)
Wendover CE Junior School, Wendover

Limericks

There once was a man from Ukraine
Who got drunk and hijacked a train,
It flew off the track
And hit an old shack,
He swore he'd never do it again!

There once was a man from Paris
Who was once really embarrassed.
He dropped his pants
And started a rant
The poor man from Paris.

There once was a man from Vancouver,
Who got sucked straight up the Hoover,
He got lost in the dust
And made a huge fuss,
He never got out of the Hoover.

There once was a man on a cruise,
Who drank a bit too much booze,
He took over the boat
And swapped the captain for a stoat,
It was all on the ten o'clock news!

There once was a man from Japan
Who fell in the frying pan,
He burned his face
And looked a disgrace,
That poor man from Japan.

Tom Erlandsen (10)
Wendover CE Junior School, Wendover

Tooth Fairy

In the middle of the night
When the street lights shine bright.
She comes and tiptoes on the roof
To collect your pearl-white tooth.

Georgina Kerr (8)
Wendover CE Junior School, Wendover

The Sun And Sea

Sun
The sun is as hot as an oven,
The sun is as red as burning hot lava,
The sun is as orange as an orange,
The sun is as yellow as a banana,
The sun is like a giant fireball,
The sun is as bright as the sky.

Sea
The sea is as stormy as an elephant,
The sea is as blue as the sky,
The sea is as salty as a tub of salt,
The sea is as deep as a canyon,
The sea is as powerful as a lion,
The sea is as big as the solar system.

Daniel Patton (8)
Wendover CE Junior School, Wendover

Best Friends

Best friends stick together
Best friends like each other,
Best friends treat each other well,
Best friends, when it come to secrets, don't tell.

Best friends are nearly each other,
Best friends know each other's mother,
Best friends want the future, to be good in nature.

Best friends don't say bad stuff,
Best friends admit it when they look rough,
Best friends play together, even if it's bad weather,
Best friends never let go, unless each other says so.

Amy Simpson & Jayde Paxton (10)
Wendover CE Junior School, Wendover

Fear

Fear feels like a person has been watching your every move
Making you feel more disappointed in yourself than you already are!

It tastes like gum, which has lost its taste
From chewing it over and over again.

It sounds like raindrops tapping onto the floor
For half an hour and gives you a headache.

It smells like the soot from chimneys reminding you
Of the poor children in the workhouse many years ago!

It looks like a war and a grey dawn
Over a field in the mist.

It reminds me of someone calling me from Hell
You are coming here when you die
Over and over again so that I get a really bad memory.

Aimee Grice (11)
Wendover CE Junior School, Wendover

The Cat

When the cat ran into the house
It caught sight of a mouse
As the floorboards creaked
The poor mouse squeaked
Just before it was no more.

No more is the mouse
That was once in the house
It stained Meg's dress
And it made a terrible mess!
So in came Jess
One more, that's Tess
And the cat was just no more.

Callum Lawes (10)
Wendover CE Junior School, Wendover

Beautiful Butterfly

Slowly and silently
It flies with the gentle breeze,
Flashing rainbow colours
In every direction
Wings fluttering in the air,
A little, yet beautiful butterfly.

Bou Man Lau (9)
Wendover CE Junior School, Wendover

Art

Art is messy,
Paint everywhere,
Paint on the tables,
Paint on the chairs,
Paint on the desk lids,
Paint on the door,
Paint on the ceiling,
Paint on the floor.
Everyone likes art.
What a merry caper!
There's paint all around the room,
But none on the paper!

Kate Thompson (11)
Wendover CE Junior School, Wendover

The Eagle

Her eyes twinkle in the sun
Then she takes a swallow
She blinks her eyes
And looks at the swaying water
That's reflecting in her eyes
Suddenly she swoops down like a magnet
Flinging to metal and grabs her prey.

Sarah Jane Wilkinson (9)
Wendover CE Junior School, Wendover

Poem About Fun

Fun is blue like a deep blue sea,
It reminds me of the fairground,
It tastes like a raspberry ice cream,
It smells like candyfloss,
It sounds like the birds singing in the summer,
It looks like a beautiful summer day,
It feels like the rough summer grass.

Kieran Bendix (11)
Wendover CE Junior School, Wendover

Anger

Anger is red, like a never-ending sunset,
It smells like a burning furnace,
It looks like a smoking volcano,
It feels like a depressing flame, choking me to death.

Anger reminds me of a sword, stabbing me in the chest,
It tastes like rotten tomatoes, along with mouldy cheese,
It sounds like a trumpeting horn, making me fall to my knees.

Leonora Lawrence (10)
Wendover CE Junior School, Wendover

Waterfalls

Slowing and soothing
Prancing and dancing
Spinning and springing
Faster and faster the river gets
Crashing, dashing, bashing, smashing
Zooming, booming
Flashing, gashing
Flowing, blowing
Slicing the rocks below.

Daniel Geddes (9)
Wendover CE Junior School, Wendover

Best Friends

Best friends tell you what's hot
Best friends tell you what's not,
Best friends never let you down
Best friends should have a crown,
Best friends always share
Best friends always care,
Best friends are the . . .
Best!

Lucy Sigley (9)
Wendover CE Junior School, Wendover

Anger

Anger is black and empty like frustration
Just the feel of cold dark anger will
Send a shiver down your spine.
It sounds like a constant high-pitched screech,
It tastes like a mouldy leech.
It smells like toxic sludge
It looks like a bomb ready to go off any second,
It reminds me of an everlasting grudge . . .

Nathan McCleary (11)
Wendover CE Junior School, Wendover

Darkness/Death

Darkness is black like the dead of night,
It looks like nothing will ever be right,
Darkness feels like freezing cold air
It seems that no one will ever care
It reminds me of waiting to be taken on,
Waiting . . . waiting . . . gone!

Sophie Honeyball (11)
Wendover CE Junior School, Wendover

A Waterfall

Starting from the source,
Gleaming and beaming on and on,
Then calmly spurting and flirting,
Slowly, slowly flowing constantly glowing.
Suddenly getting quicker and quicker.

Continuously growing and then blowing and throwing
Till it goes bashing and crashing, thrashing and lashing
Towards the fall, shining, whining and combining,
Then smashing and flashing down and down,
Then a sploosh and a whoosh plus a caploosh as it hits the rocks.
And into the plunge pool swirling, twirling and whirling
As it finally grows and flows outwards.

It stretches and reaches towards the end,
Then breaks out oozing as it scourges out with the sea.

Natasha Pain (9)
Wendover CE Junior School, Wendover

Laughter

Laughter is yellow like a yellow sunflower,
It reminds me of eternal power,
It feels like a bubbling sensation inside,
It tastes like chocolate as I eat it with pride.

Laughter smells of lemons off a lemon tree,
It looks like a fluffy bumblebee,
As it buzzes around totally free.

Laughter sounds
Like happy people as
They laugh with
Glee.

Jessica Timlin (11)
Wendover CE Junior School, Wendover

Anger

Anger is red like a fierce angry bear.
Anger smells like a bomb bursting into the air with rage.
Anger looks like a burning firework about to bang.
Anger feels like red-hot chilli,
Anger reminds me of a red cherry gazing into the sun.
Anger tastes like a red-hot pepper.
Anger sounds like a volcano erupting into the clear air.

Rebecca Bailey (11)
Wendover CE Junior School, Wendover

Darkness

Darkness is mahogany, like trees burnt by a fire,
It tastes like a sour lemon turned brown.
It looks like a giant storming over the land.
It smells like a city full of the plague.
It sounds like the chilling scream of the dying.
It feels like the smooth black cape of the night.
It reminds me of that space, deep inside, where there's nothing.

Rebecca Noall (11)
Wendover CE Junior School, Wendover

Curly Wurly Bar

I took my Curly Wurly bar,
Out of the packet
Wow, that gooey toffee taste,
It tasted like it was from,
Outer space.
Scrummy, yummy chocolate bar,
It definitely came from another star.
The toffee was dunked in a chocolate puddle,
All the curls have got in a muddle!

Klara Hommel (8)
Wendover CE Junior School, Wendover

Creme Egg

Out of the wrinkly wrapper
Comes a scrummy small brown egg
Lovely and creamy
When it goes in my mouth.

Like dropped cream in a chocolate puddle
Melts on your tongue
Looks like a brown hen egg
Eating it is very fun.

I nibble round the top
I want to buy them from every shop
Looks like people have skated on it
I love it, I love the taste.

Oliver Gunson (7)
Wendover CE Junior School, Wendover

Love

Love is the colour silver, waving in the waves beautifully,
Love is a golden star, glistening in the night sky,
Love reminds me of a raspberry ripple, melting in my mouth,
Love tastes as good as a Californian smoothie,
                                that has just been whipped up,
Love smells like daffodils that have just blossomed,
                                ready for the summer,
Love sounds like horses galloping across the mountains,
Love is a power that can be broken,
Love is a graceful dolphin gliding through the ocean,

The power of love, is the greatest power of all . . .
Don't break it.

Lauren Baker (11)
Wendover CE Junior School, Wendover

Dogs

A dog chased after a cat.
A dog's white, brown or golden coat.
Shining in the sunlight.
Racing along at full speed.
Jumping, running,
Playing with people, having a good time.
Having a bowl of cornflakes for breakfast,
Having a chicken pie for tea.
Having a dance when you want to with the dog.
Some dogs are mad, crazy or most plain stupid!
There are different types of dogs,
Golden retrievers,
Greyhounds,
Dalmatians,
Some small, some big, some thin and some fat.
Some racers, some sleepers, some swimmers and
Some big, chubby and lazy.

These are the dogs I like!

Joshua Davies (10)
Wendover CE Junior School, Wendover

Love

Love is like a burning flame that will never burn out,
Love reminds me of the sweet taste of a raspberry ice cream,
Love tastes like a strawberry smoothie,
Love smells like a rose just waiting to be picked,
Love sounds like your heart beating inside your body,
Love can't be seen but can only be felt,
Love feels like soft fluffy wool squashed up in my hand,
Love is the strongest feelings flowing in your body,
It's lovely, like love.

Andrew Howarth (10)
Wendover CE Junior School, Wendover

Apple

Out of the fruit bowl I take,
A yummy scrummy apple,
When I take a bite,
It sounds like a pair of feet crunching in the snow.

All the splodgy patches on the apples
All the cow's patches,
The colour as red as a cherry,
Green, as green as the lush green grass.

Occasionally a mini hole,
For a yucky, squeezy, squishy, squashy maggot,
As round as a nearly pumped-up tennis ball,
Little bumps at the top.

A little curly stalk,
At the bottom a little jaggady circle
Just like a little zigzag belt,
I love scrumdidilyumtious apples!

Annabel Taswell-Fryer (7)
Wendover CE Junior School, Wendover

Sadness

Sadness is clear like the sharp icicles
Which stab deep into your heart
Every time you think about it.

It sounds like the funeral
March where everyone you've ever
Cared about is gone.

It feels like a sharp blade
Cutting and stabbing at your stomach.

It tastes bitter when you realise that the Devil has won . . .
He's taken the one you've loved and now you're next in line.

Milly Collier (11)
Wendover CE Junior School, Wendover

Seasons Of The Year

Summer
Summer is the time when the birds sing
Summer is the time when the bells ring.

Autumn
Autumn is the time when the leaves fall
Autumn is the time when the children kick leaves when they fall

Winter
Winter is the time when you make snowballs
Winter is the time when you make snowmen.

Spring
Spring is the time when the baby lambs are born
Spring is the time when the daffodils grow.

Charlotte Dyer (9)
Wendover CE Junior School, Wendover

Time

Like the gears in a clock go tick tick-tock
The Earth moves round the sun.

It takes months for the Earth
To move round the sun.

It takes weeks for a month to pass
It takes days for a week to pass.

It takes hours for a day to pass
It takes minutes for an hour to pass.

This is the pattern of time
But can time last forever?

Thomas Robertson (11)
Wendover CE Junior School, Wendover

Maltesers

Out of the bag I take a chocolate-covered Malteser
It melts in my mouth
When I look into the bag they look like muddy raindrops.

It's very scrummy
And as crunchy as ice
It sticks to my fingers
And makes them gooey.

They're hard and smooth
When you suck them
You see delicious chocolate.

Take them outside in the bitter cold
But them and me are warm inside.

Harry Stroud (8)
Wendover CE Junior School, Wendover

The Seasons

Spring begins the year with bright green shoots
Blossoming into coloured flowers.

Summer is a relaxing season
Which stops the schools before the harvest season takes over.

In autumn the people cry, 'Harvest time! Gather the crops.'
As the rain gets more frequent.

Winter kills the last flowers
And covers the world with a white, cruel sheet of snow.

Spring begins the year again with bright green shoots
Blossoming into coloured flowers.

Orla Flynn (11)
Wendover CE Junior School, Wendover

Seasons

S ummer, winter, autumn, spring,
E very season has good things.
A utumn leaves, winter snow,
S ummer sun, spring growth.
O ver the year the changes come,
N ever running out of fun.
S easons keep on turning.

Rachel Durrant (10)
Wendover CE Junior School, Wendover

My Dad

My dad is cool,
He swims in a pool.

My dad is fat,
He almost ate the cat.

My dad is funky
But a little bit punky.

That's my dad
And that is *that!*

Amy Mayger (10)
Wendover CE Junior School, Wendover

Teachers

T edious and trite
E ach and every one are aliens in disguise
A nnoying, we all know that well
C lever, maybe, we do not know
H ead teachers rule our school
E ach and everyone of them want to rule our school
R epetitive lessons every day
S chool is a place where aliens meet every day
                              for they plan to rule the *world!*

Katie Rippington (9)
Wendover CE Junior School, Wendover

Cats

Cats arc playful,
Cats are nice,
Jumping around,
Chasing mice.

With their swishy tails,
And pointy ears,
Cats will chase birds,
They have no fear.

Fast asleep,
On their backs,
Dreaming of food,
And little snacks.

Cuddling up,
On the rug,
Sipping coffee,
From your mum's mug!

Augusta Goodchild (10)
Wendover CE Junior School, Wendover

Teachers

Teachers are hairy
Teachers are scary
While children are in a sob
Teachers are always on the job
They have cool cars
And some have pink bras
Some look nice
But are quiet like mice
They give you the cane
If you're being a pain
And you'll be dead
If you're caught sleeping in bed.

Mark Paulley (9)
Wendover CE Junior School, Wendover

Chelsea Carnall

C helsea is one of my best friends

H elping people all the time

E verybody likes her.

L etters given to her at Christmas.

S he likes singing songs

E very time we go to assembly she likes singing

'Topsy, turvy Kingdom.'

A lways kind.

C alling people up because she hasn't got her spellings!

A bout time for her to stop singing

R eally quiet when she stops talking

N ever cheeky (Not)

A ll the time she plays with friends

L ime is her favourite fruit

L emurs are her worst animals.

Eloise Kennett-Brown (9)
Wendover CE Junior School, Wendover

The Cows

One day I saw a beast,
He was looking for a feast.
Its face was blotchy and red,
And it came and ate my head!
If you see me now,
I am a headless cow.
I know what will happen to my hair,
It will be a leather chair,
It shouldn't happen please,
They should let us free,
It's time human beings let us be.

Sam Douglas (10) & Freddie Littlewood (9)
Wendover CE Junior School, Wendover

A River's Path

Trickling and dripping,
And sliding and gliding,
And swerving and curving and merging,
Blending and churning and mixing,
Seeping and weeping and deepening,
Meandering and widening and . . .

. . . Crashing and bashing and smashing!
And cutting and strutting and jutting,
And twirling and swirling and whirling,
And tumbling and bubbling and foaming,
And rolling and bowling . . .

. . . Bursting and sweeping and creeping!
Waving and pathing and smashing,
Flowing and destroying and lashing,
Tumbling and plunging and widening out . . .

Tom Band (9)
Wendover CE Junior School, Wendover

Lucy

When we first got Lucy she could fit into the palm of your hands,
She likes to chase birds and catch hairbands.

She has bright green eyes and a wet brown nose,
But when you try to take a picture of her, never does she pose.

She lies on her back day after day,
Dreaming her dreams of food and play.

She has a bushy tail and a wobbly leg,
She has sharp claws but pink padded paws.

She is my Lucy and forever she shall be!

Zoe Rogerson (9)
Wendover CE Junior School, Wendover

Giraffe

G orgeous giraffe,
  I n a desert she loves.
R unning elegantly
A way from danger as
F ar as she can go,
F inally she is
E ating fresh green leaves.

Charlotte Fisher (10)
Wendover CE Junior School, Wendover

Squash

Squash is fun
But you have to run
The ball hits the wall
Like a bullet being shot
The wall is red and white
All of that must have given you a fright
The courts are lit by glistening lights.

Edward Hart (9)
Wendover CE Junior School, Wendover

Marylebone Station

Marylebone station makes you dizzy
Marylebone station is very busy
Trains are going round your head.
You just want to get to bed.
Going round London is really cool.
You just want to stay all day.

Gregory Moir (10)
Wendover CE Junior School, Wendover

Fear

It feels like a person has been watching your every move
Making me feel more disappointed in myself than I already am.

It tastes like that numb feeling I get in my mouth
To show that there is something stressful on my mind.

It sounds like a desperate cry for help
Somewhere in the distance anonymously.

It smells like soot from chimneys
Reminding me of the poor, skinny, suffering workhouse children.

It looks like the time I complained about something
For many years yet nobody listened.

It reminds me of the war which I was not there for
So the way I think of it is so much more exaggerated in my mind.

Heather Fotheringham (10)
Wendover CE Junior School, Wendover

Death

I turn around and Death jumps out
I look around and Death's about
Standing there, giving me grief
I try to run to make our meeting brief.

Running down the alleyway
Death behind me saying I've got to pay
I don't understand what I've done wrong
He's been trying to get me for so long.

Oh no, oh dear
Death's so near
Oh dear, oh no
I have to take Death's final blow.

Simon Phipps (10)
Wendover CE Junior School, Wendover

Spots

Spots, spots everywhere
On the ceiling
On the chair
In the dog's basket
That lives over there . . .
Spots, spots everywhere.

Spirals, spirals everywhere
On the floors
On the stairs
In the fish bowl that sits
On the sideboard . . .
Spirals, spirals everywhere

Zigzags, zigzags everywhere
Some on the ladder
Some on the table
And there is one on top of the mayor!
Zigzags, zigzags everywhere!

Hannah Routledge (11)
Wendover CE Junior School, Wendover

The Tiger

He prowls along the trees,
With his jet-black stripes,
Rippling through the slight breeze,
For he has rights in the jungle,
With a growl as loud as thunder's rumble.

His coat is as bright as the sun's blaze,
Full of bravery,
In his strong gaze,
With claws as sharp as a razor,
For he is the mighty tiger.

Georgia Priestley (10)
Wendover CE Junior School, Wendover

A Lemon's Life

There once was a small lemon,
A nice little fellow was he,
Always was fair and even,
And also rather kindly.

He grew up in a friendly old village,
A small little place on the sea,
Where all the small lemons swam around,
And played with their family.

This lemon wanted to be famous,
He adored the show career,
The idea of having a normal job,
Seemed weak, feeble and mere.

So on the first night of his show,
They turned up famous, normal and mean,
So Mr Lemon turned around,
And pulled a moony at the Queen.

The crowd erupted with laughter,
The Queen found it funny as well,
But as for what happened after that,
We ain't quite able to tell.

Alex Dean (11)
Wendover CE Junior School, Wendover

Spaghetti

Spaghetti, spaghetti everywhere
Slippery, slimy everywhere,
Looks like worms
But tastes nice.

I twirl it round and round,
Then I eat it
Yum-yum!

Chloe Goddard (8)
Wendover CE Junior School, Wendover

Maltesers

Maltesers have the best smell
They persuade you to eat them
When you know you're not supposed to
When you eat them they crunch in your mouth.

I like to kick off the muddy brown chocolate
And the chocolate persuades
You to have another!
It crunches like a shiny snail's shell

It's like a miniature boulder
You can have it
On a cake with chocolate icing and snow sprinkles.

Andrew Findlay (7)
Wendover CE Junior School, Wendover

Friendship Is . . .

Friendship is like a precious stone,
                    sparkling, shining and shimmering in the summer sun.
Friendship is like a funky flower. The flower seems to fly and flutter.
Friendship is getting stronger all the time.
Friendship is like a brilliant book; you want to read on and on.
Friendship is like metallic metal, never, never breaking or bending.
Friendship is like a stained-glass window,
                                    dreamy and different colours.
Friendship is like a bouncy, bubbly, bulky stream.
Friendship is like a waterfall, always streaming never stopping
Friendship is like a flower-filled field, always beautiful
Friendship is like a dreamy different world.
Friendship is just a breath, so don't waste it.

Freya Killilea Clark (8)
Wendover CE Junior School, Wendover

Spaghetti

It's soft and squirmy
Like little worms wriggling along
I love to suck it
My mum says it makes me strong.

Spaghetti! Spaghetti! I love it
It's yummy scrummy and tastes so chewy
I love it so much
Especially the sauce ever so gooey.

It looks like a mountain
Towering up
Here's a tip
Never eat it out of a cup!

Matthew Honeyball (8)
Wendover CE Junior School, Wendover

Best Friend

A best friend is always there
For when you're feeling down,
A best friend is always there
Just for you and me.

A best friend, you can always count on
For parties and for sleepovers,
A best friend you can always see
When you want to play.

Some people have one best friend,
Some people have two
But, really, best friends are there
Just for you and me.

Amy Brownsword (9)
Wendover CE Junior School, Wendover

Anger

Anger is red like a hot sizzling sun,
Anger smells like a volcano about to explode,
Anger looks like a rocket shooting off into the sky,
Anger feels like a hard rock that won't crack,
Anger reminds me of a ball bursting into flames,
Anger tastes like a hot, juicy pepper,
Anger sounds like a rhino, thumping through the woods,
Anger will never turn into good from bad!

Zoe Moore (11)
Wendover CE Junior School, Wendover

Darkness

Darkness is black like the screeching bat at night,
It looks like the weaving done by the dead
It feels like the cold shiver rising from the trees,
It reminds me of the nightmares of the old haunted house,
It tastes like the Christmas pudding we all drool over,
It smells like cooled cobwebs cooked in vinegar,
It sounds like the waves lapping on the rocks.

Bethany Chattle (11)
Wendover CE Junior School, Wendover

The Waterfall

Water gushing and flushing and rushing
Crashing through rocks
Splashing over the edge
Roaring as it rushes down the fall
Gushing in the waterfall
Flowing down
Lower and lower
Flushing into the pool.

Jonathan Rogers (8)
Wendover CE Junior School, Wendover

Dear Miss Emmett

Dear Miss Emmett
Don't even ask me how my brother got locked out,
The key just suddenly turned and he was outside.
I wasn't even there when it happened, I just found him now.

It's amazing how time flies by,
I wasn't hiding in the cloakroom,
I was just tidying up.
It was only a minute ago when we came in.
I can't believe the whole literacy lesson has gone by.

Why would I trip up Mr George?
You must think I want to be expelled.
Mr George tripped over all by himself.
It was nothing to do with me.

I didn't scribble on the blackboard
It was already there when I went in.
Honestly, I'm innocent.
I didn't do any of these things.
(Except for all of them. Don't tell Mr George that!)

Eleanor Claringbold (9)
Wendover CE Junior School, Wendover

Love

Love is the colour of pink, glistening in the moonlight,
It is like a burning flame that will never burn out,
Reminding me of a diary that is waiting to be opened,
It tastes like a strawberry smoothie just picked off a bush,
Smelling like the sweet, sweet red rose petals,
Love sounds like the beating of your heart
Gradually getting faster and faster
Love cannot be seen, only felt
Feeling like your whole body will fly away
Unless someone is holding onto you
That's my feeling of love.

Shannon Kitson (10)
Wendover CE Junior School, Wendover

Fear

Fear is black like a vampire bat
It feels like sticky syrup on top of a pancake
It tastes like bitter lime, which is not ripe
It sounds like a little girl screaming really loudly
It looks like cobwebs but not with a spider
It reminds me of a dark night with danger ahead.

Hannah Baines (11)
Wendover CE Junior School, Wendover

Carrots

Carrots, carrots
Munch, munch, munch
I always have them with my lunch

Carrots, carrots
Rabbits like them too
I always have them in my stew.

Carrots, carrots
They're so nice
I always have them with my rice.

Milly Douglas (7)
Wendover CE Junior School, Wendover

Love

Love is red, like cherry-coloured chocolate
It smells like pancakes with golden syrup.
It feels like butterflies in the pit of my stomach.
It reminds me of why I live
It sounds like angels singing above
It tastes like the sensation of when chocolate melts in your mouth
It looks like the great sight of the rainforest.

Jack Brownsword (11)
Wendover CE Junior School, Wendover

Strawberries

Strawberries are so yum in my tum,
I cannot exist without them,
Strawberries are as red as a pen,
But, of course, when the pen is red.
There's no more strawberries left now,
So I shut the door and say,
'That's the end of them!'

Sarah Baughan (8)
Wendover CE Junior School, Wendover

Haribo

So sugary,
So sweet,
So chewy it makes you go crazy,
It can keep you active,
The taste of it is so sweet
That you can't believe
It is so delicious.

Harry Fisher (7)
Wendover CE Junior School, Wendover

Ice Cream

Ice cream has a cold icy taste
You lick it with your tongue on your face,
There are different flavours
For example there is:
Snowy, white vanilla
Peachy, pink strawberry
Brown, muddy chocolate
And greeny, grass mint,
But my favourite's choc chip!

Rebecca Mitton (8)
Wendover CE Junior School, Wendover

The Course Of A River

Trickling and dripping,
And flowing and slipping,
Faster and faster,
And off it goes.

Crashing and bashing and flashing,
And bubbling and troubling,
And ripping and chipping,
And swirling and twirling.

Rushing through the teeny small gap,
Getting faster and faster like saying a rap,
Gets eager and eager to get to the end,
There it goes, round the bend.

Caitlin McGowan (9)
Wendover CE Junior School, Wendover

Fruit Salad

I love to eat it with greed,
The grapes roll in my tum,
The meringue is as white as snow,
The juice of the raspberries sticks to my throat,
I wish I could have tons of it,
So creamy,
I let the cream sink down my throat,
So lovely, just waiting to be eaten,
I think it knows I love it!
I just love them. The plum, the raspberry,
The *meringue!*
Ah, fruit salad!

Sam Bailey (8)
Wendover CE Junior School, Wendover

Chocolate Cake

It made me fly,
I flew right across the sky.
It tickled me inside,
I went to hide.
I took the cake with me,
I was hiding under the chocolate tree.
She came out and said,
'Do you want some more?'
I went popping mad.
How many cakes do you have?
I had lots and lots,
Give me some more!
I'll eat them up before you can say sure!

Jamie Nightingale (8)
Wendover CE Junior School, Wendover

Kenning

Little walker
Tiny talker
Creeper squeaker
Naughty peeper
Eating cheese
Begs please
Runs away
In the hay.

Magic wings
Little tings,
Lovely and pink
Disappears when you blink.

Grace Blackman (8)
Wendover CE Junior School, Wendover

Fish

When I take the fish out of the bog,
I love to dig my teeth into it
I feel the soft, white snow on my teeth.
As I happily smile.
When I swallow the brilliant fish,
I think of where it's been.
Diving in and out of the waves,
Coming nearer and nearer to the shore.

Nick Dean (8)
Wendover CE Junior School, Wendover

Mash

Mash, mash with my fork,
Hot in my mouth,
As yellow as a buttercup,
It's like a miniature rocky mountain.

As big as a pie,
Smashy, mashy,
Lovely to eat,
I like my mash.

Sam Page (8)
Wendover CE Junior School, Wendover

My Mum

Mummy you're fantastic
And good at gymnastics
You are the one who is very sweet
And you are very hard to beat
You are kind and really warm
But what I like about you the most
Is you loved me before I was born.

Helen Twomey (9)
Wendover CE Junior School, Wendover

The River's Course

It starts with a swirl,
And a tiny twirl,
It starts with a steady ease,
It carries its water past the trees
Its water's now crystal-clear,
And it can hear,
It's close to the sea
It's now happy with glee.

But now it's at the edge of the mountain,
It makes a spray of a fountain,
It starts splashing,
And badly bashing,
Then comes the drop,
There happens no plop,
But a splash,
And a same-sized bash . . .

Then it carries on lapping to get to the end,
Still going faster and faster it goes round the bends,
Then it starts pounding,
And desperately bounding,
Splashing its shiny water over the sides,
It doesn't glide but cleverly guides,
Its fantastic, shiny water is now happy with glee,
For it has now finally reached freedom, the sea.

Katie Stewart (9)
Wendover CE Junior School, Wendover

Acrostic Poem

L ovely Lee learns lots,
E ager to go out and play,
E ager to work hard,
   However, he can be a pain.

Lee Howarth (8)
Wendover CE Junior School, Wendover

Danger

Anger is red, stained in blood
It will make you want to kill your best bud
It sounds like a headache beating on your skull
Or the sound of a demented seagull
It tastes of layers of thick, black smoke
That gives you pain and makes you choke
It looks like a never-ending ball of misery
You'll wish it never happened, it will make you dizzy
It feels like being toasted on a fire
It will make you think everyone's a liar
It will remind you of your worst memories
It brings hatred, it brings enemies
It smells like a mouldy, decapitated head
Anger is like stained blood, anger is red.

Jack Bedwell (10)
Wendover CE Junior School, Wendover

The Diners In The Kitchen

Our dog Meg
Ate the egg
Our dog Nicole
Ate the swiss roll
Our dog Helen
Ate the melon
Our dog Sam
Ate the ham
Our dog Ben
Ate the hen
Our dog Tom
Ate the bonbon.

Megan Vigor (9)
Wendover CE Junior School, Wendover

Happiness

Happiness is the colour of rosy pink
Like the colour of our lips when we smile.

It feels like the soft touch of silk
Dribbling down your body.

It sounds like a hummingbird
Flying up to the heavens above.

It tastes like the melting sensation
Of chocolate in your mouth.

It smells like the scent of the flowers
And glorious food in country houses.

It looks like the perfect roses beneath us
And the way our hair flutters in the water.

It reminds me of the reason of life.

Rebecca Hunt (11)
Wendover CE Junior School, Wendover

Happiness

Happiness is light blue,
Like the colour of the sky when there are no clouds.

It feels like a flame in my heart.
It sounds like the church bells ringing.

It smells like the love in one another's hearts.
It tastes like the wind running through my hair.

It looks like the joy when someone says yes.
It reminds me of my dog called Poppy whom I loved very much.

Jasmine Newman (11)
Wendover CE Junior School, Wendover

Wolf Poem

Monday's child is nice and sour
Tuesday's child goes nice with flour
Wednesday's child is easy to bake
Thursday's child is a piece of cake
Friday's child goes good with oil
Saturday's child is good to boil
Sunday's child is very delicious
Even though it is a little vicious.

Arran Stewart (9)
Wendover CE Junior School, Wendover

Waterfall

Crashing and bashing and crashing
Ripping and splashing and twirling
Burying and boiling and tumbling
Swirling and sparkling and rumbling
Lashing and thrashing and destroying
Popping and moping
Whirling and twirling after bends
Tossing and bossing the river flow.

Nicholas Kent (8)
Wendover CE Junior School, Wendover

My Pet Jim

My pet Jim is a smelly thing
And is greedy and eats a whole baked beans tin.
He has a round tummy and eats your tea
And because he is so lazy
He can't move his feet.
I don't understand he is not my pet
I must get him to the vet.

Krista Hamlyn (8)
Wendover CE Junior School, Wendover

Fun!

Fun is yellow like the warm summer sun,
Fun tastes like chocolate, melting in your mouth,
Fun feels like fur, all warm and soft,
Fun sounds like music, relaxing and smooth,
Fun looks like happy children playing in the woods,
Fun reminds you of a colourful rug.

Katrina Wilton (11)
Wendover CE Junior School, Wendover

Miss Emmett

Miss Emmett is fun and really great,
She cares for you like you were her own child.
Miss Emmett will listen when you need to speak,
She'll never let you down.

Miss Emmett is very tall,
She also might be a bit scary,
Miss Emmett is kind, she really is,
She's also very bold.

Chloe Hinchliffe (9)
Wendover CE Junior School, Wendover

Waterfall

Rushing and gushing and slushing,
Lapping and slapping,
Whirling and twirling and swirling,
Ripping and dripping,
Dashing and crashing and splashing,
Bashing and smashing,
Twisting and sloshing and glistening,
Sprinkling and twinkling.

Naomi Garner (8)
Wendover CE Junior School, Wendover

Sadness

Sadness is as black as a cold, empty sky,
It sounds like silence; time just going on and on,
It feels like a hard sea wind, digging deep and scarring your skin.
It smells like a damp ditch, where you've been stabbed and left to die
It tastes like watching your enemy take sweet victory,
It looks like an empty graveyard, all by yourself,
Reminding you, it's always there trying to steal the
only happiness left in your soul
Only left with sadness.

Beth Ivory (11)
Wendover CE Junior School, Wendover

Fear

Fear is black, like the darkest of darkness.
It looks like a tunnel with no end to it.
It smells like rotten plastic burning.
It feels like emptiness where there should be happiness.
It reminds me of death with no life beyond.

Vicky Smith (11)
Wendover CE Junior School, Wendover

Hunger

Hunger is yellow, like dying crops in a field
It looks like a lone soldier, fighting for survival.
It feels like an emptiness feeding inside you.
It sounds like a rumbling, lasting forever
It tastes like the bitterness of war in the world.
It smells like something evil from the earth.
It reminds me of famine, caused by the war.

Aaron Roberts (11)
Wendover CE Junior School, Wendover

Portraits

P ictures and photos all over the walls, in your photo albums
and in art galleries.

O ver everywhere I go, they're stuck glaring at me,
I feel like they're just like me.

R ound and round all around me I see pictures all over the city.

T all and short, round and square, pictures are everywhere.

R eady, steady, here you go to the art galleries all over the world

A ll around you can see all sorts of portraits wall to wall
different kinds of pictures.

I see lots of pictures upside down and all around

T rying to escape but have no chance, smashing all
the glass, saying 'Help me, help!'

S traight lines, diagonal lines all over the pictures making
paths to run away.

Henna Akhtar (11)
William Austin Junior School, Luton

A Monkey

I can see the Amazon rainforest
I can see the animals running
I can see the lorries coming
I can see the trees being knocked down
I feel scared
I feel I don't know where to go
I can hear noise pollution
I can hear trees falling
I can hear the animals screaming.

Emily Ward (11)
William Austin Junior School, Luton

War

I want to see clouds not bombers in the sky.
I want to see fresh green grass not rubble on the floor.
I want to see children happy instead of crying for their mothers.
I want to see people alive not dead on the ground.
I feel sad, I feel angry with Hitler for doing all this
I want to light a candle for the prime minister
                                        and send him a peaceful prayer
We want to win, we have to win the war for
                        the innocent people who died during air raids.

Zahra Ilyas (11)
William Austin Junior School, Luton

Rivers

R ivers are waters that race down to the sea at a very fast speed.
I n rivers there may be litter, which stinks so much.
V ery few people have seen the astonishing and
                                        amazing sight of a river
E very day people fish in the river for fun
R ain fills up the rivers and the rivers pass the water to the seas
S unny weather evaporates the water.

Shafaqat Ali (10)
William Austin Junior School, Luton

Rivers

R ivers go down hills and into seas
I n the sea there are not many trees
V ery little birds sit in a river and drink
E veryone sits and thinks
R ivers are so good they make you blink.

Haseeb Akhmed (10)
William Austin Junior School, Luton

The War

S urrounded, I feel terrified

O verhead bombs are fired, destruction is all around,

L ighting up the sky bullets rip flesh and bone,

D eath and destruction is all around,

I t takes my breath away, the sight of death,

E very muscle exhausted, as cannons rip the sky,

R etreat! Retreat!

Ben Rollins (11)
William Austin Junior School, Luton

Pyramids

Pyramids
I am so smooth
And shiny as bright
As the sun protecting
Pharaohs every day! I see
Them lying everywhere and could
Feel sorrow and sadness everywhere
Inside me. I hear people screaming and
Crying because their loved ones had *died!*

Afeefa Anwar (11)
William Austin Junior School, Luton

Rivers

R ivers have natural water with pure things in it

I n the water they have lovely creatures

V arieties of animals in the river love swimming

E veryone goes to the river to drink

R ivers have lots of riots like sharks eating fish

S aying that makes me want to go to the river with riots
and a variety of animals.

Sharaz Khan (11)
William Austin Junior School, Luton

Rivers

The singing of the water simmers,
The hoof beats of a white horse,
Pearl doves screeching high above me,
People treading on the shores.

The features of a silhouette walking,
On the sun-setted horizon beach.
A dolphin flipping on the surface waters,
So far, no one can reach.

The warming breeze passing just beside me,
The soft blue water trickling down my roots,
Although it's raining a soft shower of droplets
No one dare wear boots!

Sanya Wadud (11)
William Austin Junior School, Luton

Save The Animals

To see a world in grain and sand,
Hold infinity in the palm of your hand.
For the silver swan who had no note,
When death approached it unlocked her throat.
Hurt no living thing,
No moth with a dusty wing.
Where in the jungles near and far,
Man-devouring tigers are.
Send those away,
Who wish not to obey.
We will keep our faith with us,
And hope no one betrays us.

Tahira Iqbal (10)
William Austin Junior School, Luton

Being A Christian

I am a Christian as you see,
I know I love Jesus and Jesus loves me
We all love each other we're like one,
We are praising the Holy God and Mighty One.
A Christian for Jesus I'm proud to be,
A soldier of the cross of love and purity.
I'll be obedient, be pure, and be true,
Be kind; be respectful in all that I do.
I'll be attentive, be helpful, and be cheerful,
Be thoughtful; be reverent for God is everywhere.
I see Jesus in my life,
He is the one that makes it right.
He is always in my heart,
And he is at the top of the chart.

Shanaide Robinson (11)
William Austin Junior School, Luton

Artistic!

I can feel the paint in my hands
All messy and splodgy, being painted on a big piece of paper.
I can feel the pencil in my hand working as hard as it can.

I can hear my mind thinking as quickly as it can . . .
I can hear the ideas going through my mind.
This is what I hear.

I can see a beautiful picture all ready to be put up
And full of different colours.
Red, yellow and blue.
I can see myself as proud as I can be.

I am an artist.

Sara Naeem (10)
William Austin Junior School, Luton

Work

Work, work, work
Everyone you have spare time for work
Sing about or even read a book or two.
I know you can, you could do it too.

People from all around the world are working hard.
You could work like them and make a card.
Or even make a tart for your love hearts.

Work, work, work
Everyone you have spare time for work
Sing about or even read a book or two
I know you can, you could do it too.

Hey do you know Mr Ward said work for your life
And never give up, study harder
And join in some fun making plants with your father.

Majda Khan (11)
William Austin Junior School, Luton

The Wonderful World Of The Forest

I can see trees, bees and animals
Also plants everywhere.
To flying snakes and green birds
I can feel the wood,
Strong, tall trees and squelching mud beneath my feet.
Unusual creatures hiding, watching me, wondering.
I can hear squawking birds and hissing sssnakesss
Animals singing and dancing to attract the other mates.

Natasha Mamenemuno (10)
William Austin Junior School, Luton